harlem
STYLE

RODERICK N. SHADE

AND JORGE S. ARANGO

STYLE

DESIGNING FOR THE NEW URBAN AESTHETIC

PHOTOGRAPHY BY PETER MADERO

WITH A FOREWORD BY STAR JONES

STEWART, TABORI & CHANG

NEW YORK

747.09747
SH12

Unless otherwise indicated, all photographs are by Peter Madero.
Additional photo credits appear on page 175, which shall be
considered an extension of this page.

Assistant Stylists: Tracy Blanks and Kenneth Baldwin

Published in 2002 by
STEWART, TABORI & CHANG
A Company of La Martinière Groupe
115 West 18th Street
New York, NY 10011

Export Sales to all countries except Canada, France,
and French-speaking Switzerland:
Thames and Hudson Ltd.
181A High Holborn
London, WC1V 7QX
England

Canadian Distribution:
Canadian Manda Group
One Atlantic Avenue, Suite 105
Toronto, Ontario M6K 3E7
Canada

Library of Congress Cataloging-in-Publication Data
Shade, Roderick N.
Harlem style / Roderick N. Shade and Jorge S. Arango.
p. cm.
Includes bibliographical references.
ISBN 1-58479-091-1
1. Interior decoration—New York (State)—New York. 2. Harlem (New York, N.Y.)
3. Multiculturalism in interior decoration. I. Arango, Jorge S. II. Title.

NK2011.N48 S5 2002
747'.09747'1—dc21   2002021602

The text of this book was composed in The Mix.

Printed in Japan by Toppan Printing

10 9 8 7 6 5 4 3 2 1

First Printing

OPPOSITE: **African chair, sculpture
and textiles at Mosaic Antique and
Contemporary Design in New York.**
TITLE PAGE: **Marc Anderson's
renovated church in East Harlem.**
CONTENTS PAGE: **Story Stones
fabric by Donghia Furniture/
Textiles Ltd.**

For my father, Noble W. Shade.

contents

FOREWORD

Harlem to me is about all things that should be reflected in the perfectly designed home—style, class, and history; and home should be a place of comfort and welcome. I was born in Badin, North Carolina, and raised both there and in Trenton, New Jersey. I now live in a penthouse in New York City and a wooded retreat in East Hampton, NY. But those are my homes. I wanted a designer who has a vision of the way my "home" should look, not how my "house" should look.

I first met Roderick Shade when I began thinking about renovating my new penthouse apartment. My friend Karol DeWolfe at *Traditional Home* magazine recommended him to me. It was obvious why when I started to see evidence of his work on other projects—his attention to detail, impeccable taste, sense of history, and the simple but profound principles of design, which he calls "Harlem Style."

When I was a young girl, someone once told me that I needed to learn how not to "rock the boat" and things would come to me much easier. I told my mother what this (obviously misguided) individual had said and her response was: "Baby, if you ain't in the boat, turn the boat over!" That's the way I feel about stuffy design rules. I'm the author of the only dictionary that defines me, and in Roderick's approach to design, I've found a way to define my surroundings. His principles of Harlem Style are helping me express myself in my home.

To me, style really must express substance. Harlem Style is about finding and portraying in your environs what's important to you. As Roderick and I design my homes, these principles are a vehicle for creating an atmosphere that reflects who I am and what is important to me. For example, I am blessed that I have always had a mother and father who believe in me. I had the most wonderful upbringing from two of the kindest human beings on the planet. I never knew a day growing up when my parents didn't say something encouraging. I want that reflected in my home. I was never compared to other children. I was just me and encouraged to be me. That individuality has to be visible in my personal space. My mom taught me responsibility, self-esteem, and encouraged me to shine brightly. . .and I thank her everyday. I don't like to end the day without calling to laugh with my mom about something. So, humor and wit must be evident in my home. Even now, my parents never end a conversation with their children without saying, "I love you." My home must exude love.

And, at the same time, I want decadent elegance. My home also needs to be a romantic fantasy retreat, a place where no personal indulgence is out of place.

The elements of Harlem Style make "home" a fabulous setting in which to live out your dreams. Learn from it how to write your own personal dictionary of style.

STAR JONES

INTRODUCTION

The word Harlem today has lost virtually all connection to its origins. It is, of course, Dutch, and refers to the town of Haarlem in the Netherlands, seat of a very important school of northern European baroque art where the great painters Franz Hals and Jacob van Ruisdael plied their trade. It was natural that the Dutch, who first established New Amsterdam as a port city, would name neighborhoods after familiar locales back home, and that the English, who came after them, would change or corrupt those names.

So New Amsterdam became New York, and Haarlem became Harlem. Yet who nowadays, other than a curator of seventeenth-century Dutch painting, would leap instinctively to the association with Hals or Ruisdael before any other?

A casual canvassing of friends and acquaintances of many races and backgrounds reveals that practically no one makes the Dutch association unless specifically prompted; not even citizens of Holland or nearby Belgium, who you might reasonably have expected to venture a passing familiarity with the Haarlem that gave Harlem its name.

Instead, these are the most prevalent associations Harlem elicits in the contemporary collective consciousness: Great Northern Migration, Black Renaissance, jazz and blues, the Cotton Club, the Apollo Theater, soul, gangsters, black folks, spats and style, Bessie Smith, Josephine Baker, collard greens, "take the A Train," din, noise, activity, pulsating, rhythmic, inventive, brownstones, glamorous buildings, nightlife, taboo, "way" uptown, "zooted" up for the night,

open fire hydrants on hot summer days, double-Dutch jump-roping, rich ethnic and cultural diversity, trains roaring by, the El zigzagging, churches, Panama hats, panache, writers, artists, culture, the shuffle, the cake-walk, gambling and drugs, crime, danger, gangs, fine but run-down Victorian buildings, faded grandeur, overlooked, political activism, Malcolm X, Martin Luther King, Jr., Adam Clayton Powell, the Hotel Theresa, community, pride, Ossie Davis and Ruby Dee, gentrification, the big open market, kente and color, refuge, vibrant life, "the real birth of cool," basketball on hot asphalt...and, finally, the office of former President Bill Clinton.

These associations trace a rich and complex trajectory through boom times and bum times, opulence, dilapidation, and rebirth. The quaint Haarlem of the Dutch settlers has evolved, semantically speaking, into an experience and state of mind that is urban, artistic, cultured, activist, and black.

So how does this translate into a decorative style? Easily. Harlem Style is at heart contemporary urban style—that is, modern, worldly, fashionable, hip—but with a distinct and identifiable ethnic twist. That twist is often quite apparent, as when a designer mixes in African masks or textiles with sleek furnishings. But it also may be very subliminally introduced—by grass cloth on a wall or Chinese porcelain garden stools used as end tables. Starting with an earthy neutral palette, it creates interest by blending many design styles, juxtaposing primitive textures with modern synthetic ones, and adding objects and accessories that speak to the melting pot of cultures and peoples that make up the modern city. And it evolves as cities do, absorbing important new developments in art, design, and technology to arrive each time at a statement that is unique, fresh, and elegant.

Probably more than any urban center, Harlem has undergone continuous and momentous evolution. Indeed, many of the impressions of Harlem that people cling to no longer have currency. R&B and hip hop have replaced jazz as the predominant music of this (or, arguably, any) area; the El is long gone; Bessie Smith, Josephine Baker, Dr. King, and Malcolm X have left us; and crime and drugs, as inescapable here as in even the quietest American suburb, are far more prevalent in other boroughs of New York than on the streets of Harlem.

Yet the Apollo Theater is once again a vibrant showcase for African-American entertainment. There is abundant nightlife. The Studio Museum in Harlem has become the place to see the hottest up-and-coming visual artists in any medium. And writers, photographers, painters, designers, and sculptors of every stripe are still there in every precinct of the neighborhood. The venerable Stanford White residences along Striver's Row (138th and 139th Streets) and dignified facades around Mount Morris Park, Sugar Hill, Convent Avenue, Jumel Terrace, and other notable enclaves, still stand, imparting a timeless and stolid elegance. There is kente and color at the open-air Malcolm Shabazz Harlem Market.

And now there is much more—streets abuzz with a rich sprinkling of Caribbeans, Hispanics, African immigrants, and whites. The new offices of William Jefferson Clinton, planned and outfitted by a black designer, look out on 125th Street. Sophistication mingles with streetwise savvy. There are Latin groceries, a milliner and haute couture boutiques, a Body Shop, a Starbucks.

Harlem's trajectory continues along its storied and celebrated path, a path paved in the first Harlem Renaissance, and now leading the way into a new millennium.

RODERICK N. SHADE

PREVIOUS PAGE: **Exterior of a Harlem interior design shop, circa 1926.**

the new urban aesthetic

harlem
CAPITAL OF BLACK AMERICA

Prior to the first Harlem Renaissance, which occurred in the first third of the twentieth century, this far-northern tract of Manhattan—distinguished by banks of Victorian brownstones facing graceful, tree-lined boulevards, as well as pre-war buildings and architecturally distinct tenements—had been populated successively by Germans, Irish, European Jews, and then African Americans. Records show the first blacks moved to Harlem in 1905, in the midst of a severe national depression and overbuilding in the neighborhood. A murder in an apartment at 31 West 133rd Street had rendered that address virtually unrentable. The landlord enlisted the help of Philip A. Payton, a black realtor, who recruited black tenants willing to pay $5 more a month than any white. Overpayment of rent, unfortunately, was not an uncommon practice among blacks. Despite the fact that the vast majority

LEFT: **Stanford White houses on Striver's Row, West 139th Street between 7th and 8th Avenue, Harlem, 1920s.**
PREVIOUS PAGE: **Roderick Shade's design for a guest room in the Harlem United Showhouse in 1998.**

of African Americans earned far less than whites, the Urban League reported that 48 percent of Harlemites spent twice as much of their income on rent as white New Yorkers in 1927, the height of the Harlem Renaissance, when the neighborhood was almost exclusively black.

White Harlemites were appalled that the first door was open to blacks at 133rd Street. They called for repelling "the black hordes," going so far as to propose a 24-foot-high fence at 136th Street to mark their boundary. But the great Northern Migration was on, from lower Manhattan, where Americans of African descent had resided since before the Revolutionary War and, more significantly, from the rural Jim Crow South. Between the World Wars, more than two million black Americans migrated from the South, a significant number of them to Harlem. By 1920, the influx had swelled the confines of "the black belt" from a few square blocks in the low 130s between Fifth and Seventh Avenue, to a huge swath that extended from 130th Street to 145th, and from Madison to Eighth Avenue.

As they made a new home, they created a new culture: the Harlem Renaissance. By the mid-1920s, Harlem had become the capital of black America, prompting the poet and novelist Arna Bontemps to exclaim, "In some places the autumn of 1924 may have been an unremarkable season. In Harlem, it was like a foretaste of paradise."

THE HARLEM RENAISSANCE AND MODERNISM

The Northern Migration coincided with various historical and social factors that catapulted African-American culture to unprecedented heights of popularity and fashion. For one, European modernism had been born. So-called "primitivism" had begun with Gauguin and Matisse, who were among the first painters to use a visual vocabulary influenced by African forms in their art. But it was Picasso who exploded onto the scene with these forms and sent the art world reeling. His *Les Demoiselles d'Avignon,* painted in 1907, announced cubism in the loudest, brashest possible terms. The scholar and critic Henry Louis Gates Jr. has called that painting "a testament to the shaping influence of African sculpture and to the central role that African art played in the creation of modernism." Gris, Braque, Modigliani, and Brancusi, among others, took up the modernist mantle.

Modernism brought long-overdue recognition to African art. At the time, Duke Ellington wryly noted, "The Europeans who went to Africa came back with 'modern' art. What is more African than a Picasso?"

Another important factor that shaped the Harlem Renaissance was black participation in the military. Despite segregation in the armed services, the onset of World War I also provided a measure of enhanced self-esteem among black Americans. In her 1987 introduction to The Studio Museum in Harlem's exhibition catalog for *Harlem Renaissance: Art of Black America,* then-director Mary Schmidt Campbell wrote: "For the Black infantrymen who fought overseas, the war provided an opportunity to experience firsthand the rising importance of African cultures and to learn about the burgeoning popularity of negritude, a philosophy created by African and Caribbean poets that promoted the unity and beauty of peoples of African descent."

Black regiments distinguished themselves on the frontlines of battle, while controversy seethed about segregated training and commissioning of black officers and about black soldiers being sent into the field only to man mess tents. In his acclaimed history of the Harlem Renaissance, *When Harlem Was in Vogue,* David Levering Lewis points out that the 369th Infantry Regiment—comprised primarily of Harlem's Fifteenth National Guard Regiment and dubbed the "Hell Fighters" for its demonstration of bravery and valor—became the only American unit awarded France's *Croix de Guerre* and the regiment chosen by the French High Command "to lead the march to the Rhine." Recounting the 369th's triumphal homecoming march, led by Colonel William Hayward up Fifth Avenue to Harlem on February 17, 1919, Lewis wrote: "The Hell Fighters were home. They had come, as thousands of other returning Afro-American soldiers came, with a music, a lifestyle, and a dignity new to the nation—and soon to pervade it."

The Hell Fighters' regiment band, led by Big Jim Europe, had mesmerized audiences in France, Belgium, and Britain with this new, soulful sound. Jazz was the first truly American avant-garde art form and it was, undeniably, black. "You could remove the white elements—the French quadrilles, the Mexican military rhythms, the Italian melodies—and the music would still recognizably be jazz," wrote Laurence Bergreen. "But if you removed the black elements—the emphasis on improvisation, the polyphony, the complex rhythms, not to mention the all-important attitude that music was part of daily life—the remainder would not be jazz." Duke Ellington pronounced it "the only music that is able to describe the present period in the history of the world."

While modernism crossed the Atlantic from east to west, jazz moved west to east. Its repercussions were global. Paris and Harlem became twin stars in this new constellation, with black musicians and performers moving fluidly between the two cities. Black revues like "Shuffle Along" sparked a rage for new forms of dance inspired by the syncopated sounds of jazz—the cakewalk, the turkey trot,

In this undated view of the Reverend George Wilson Becton's sitting room on 120th Street, we begin to notice the influence of art deco in the piano lamp and the metal grillwork, as well as a more pronounced feeling of openness, with large sections of floor and wall left unadorned except for parquet pattern underfoot and the wallpaper.

the Charleston. Jazz embodied the progressive face America wished to show Europe, and the black culture from which it had sprung was suddenly embraced by American whites. "Maybe these Nordics at last have tuned in on our wavelength," mused the Harlem Renaissance writer Rudolph Fisher in the *American Mercury* in 1927.

The confluence of all these factors—the Northern Migration, the pride of black military participation in World War I, white embrace of black musical culture, as well as economic, educational, and political progress—led to positive ethnic affirmation among Americans of African descent that flowered irreversibly in Harlem. The NAACP was founded in 1909, the Urban League in 1910. Marcus Garvey and his Universal Negro Improvement Association pioneered African nationalism. Painters like Palmer Hayden, William H. Johnson and, most of all, Aaron Douglas, consciously eschewed traditional white European forms of artistic expression in favor of a more authentically African style. Writers such as Zora Neal Hurston championed the artistic validity of the African-American experience.

And Langston Hughes published his essay "The Negro Artist and the Racial Mountain" in which he asked, almost incredulously, "Why should I want to be white? I am a Negro—and beautiful!"

There was no turning back.

Mrs. Haughey's sitting room at Manhattan Avenue and 117th Street in 1898, typifies the cluttered approach to decoration of the Victorian era. Though the room contains ethnic elements— an Egyptian floor cushion and a Japanese screen— they are practically lost in a sea of gilt frames, tassels, and European furnishings.

THE HEIGHT OF FASHION

Langston Hughes compared Harlem to a "great magnet for the Negro intellectual, pulling him from everywhere." This was certainly true, but the pull of that magnet proved equally irresistible to white society. "Negro stock is going up," wrote Rudolph Fisher in the *American Mercury* in 1927, "and everybody's buying."

The pied piper of this white movement was novelist, photographer, and former music critic of *The New York Times,* Carl Van Vechten, who told Hughes that "...indubitably now is the psychological moment when everything chic is Negro." In his own apartment at 150 West 55th Street, he hosted mixed-race parties that provided black artists with valuable introductions to what Zora Neal Hurston called "Negrotarians," whites like editor Max Eastman, publisher Alfred Knopf, and *Vanity Fair*'s Frank Crowninshield who supported the New Negro Movement.

But Van Vechten also possessed an acute radar for fashion, and his interests in black culture extended well beyond the literary and artistic. He quickly became a habitué of Jungle Alley, a stretch of 133rd Street that boasted the highest concentration of jazz clubs in the neighborhood, as well as the high-toned Cotton Club, and the bawdy entertainments of the speakeasies and rent parties. He was a regular visitor at the posh literary salons held at A'Lelia Walker's Dark Tower and at the considerably lower-brow Niggerati Manor, a rooming house for writers like Hurston, Hughes, Wallace Thurman, and the flamboyantly homosexual artist, writer, and bohemian Richard Bruce Nugent, who covered the walls with paintings of bright phalluses. Van Vechten brought with him all of Manhattan's high society: Princess Violette Murat, Cecil Beaton, Gertrude Vanderbilt Whitney, Otto Kahn, Lady Mountbatten, Libby Holman, Beatrice Lilly, Muriel Draper, and scores of others. So ubiquitous was Van Vechten on the Harlem social scene that going uptown became known as "van vechtening" around.

This interior of Harlem's famed Lenox Lounge, photographed by James VanDerZee, c. 1940s, shows the typical art deco accents of the day, and the popular black-and-white checkered floors common in many nightclubs of the Harlem Renaissance period.

Suddenly, the parlors of Park Avenue high society and the living rooms of the Greenwich Village intellectuals and literati enthusiastically welcomed what was viewed as the most promising new literary and artistic milieu in America. Hughes, Hurston, the effete Alain Locke, and the poet Countee Cullen: black painters, composers, and musicians attended soirées at the most fashionable Upper East Side homes and more cerebral gatherings downtown, mingling with people like Jascha Heifetz, Ethel Barrymore, and Fannie Hurst. Impresarios like Florenz Ziegfeld and writers like Heywood Broun went uptown, shrewdly scanning the party scene for new black talent, or spending evenings with the prominent black intellectuals who David Levering Lewis called the "midwives of the Harlem Renaissance," people like James Weldon Johnson and Walter White.

"It was a period," recalled Langston Hughes in *The Big Sea*, "when, at almost every Harlem upper-crust dance or party, one would be introduced to various distinguished White celebrities there as guests. It was a period when almost any Harlem Negro of any social importance at all would be likely to say casually: 'As I was remarking the other day to Heywood—,' meaning Heywood Broun. Or: 'As I said to George—,' referring to George Gershwin. It was a period when local and visiting royalty were not at all uncommon in Harlem…It was the period when the Negro was in vogue."

In Paris, Eileen Gray was an early champion of the new eclecticism that married ethnic art and ornament with the modern glamour of the Jazz Age. In this living room from 1933, she mixed African furniture and hides with modern art and furnishings, and set her composition against walls covered in silver leaf.

THE BIRTH OF HARLEM STYLE

The Northern Migration, modernism, jazz, and a new American black identity had ramifications in interior design as well. The Harlem Renaissance gave birth to a new kind of eclecticism.

Victorian eclecticism had grown largely from an anthropological impulse. Style makers of that era amassed artifacts of other cultures and exhibited them as curiosities amid fine European and American antiques. Non-European cultures were present, but they did not inform Victorian style. (Chinoiserie was a noticeable exception.)

Modernism, with its appreciation of African form, changed that. It was evident in art, but also in furnishings. Art deco, though streamlined and metropolitan in appearance, actually borrowed prodigiously from African sculptural shapes and from the simplicity of line in African design. Natural materials like grasses and bamboo, as well as a very African predilection for mixing wood, metal, and stone, became fashionable. Formal brocades, tapestries, and chintzes gave way to coarser weaves and textures. And African art and artifacts were no longer exhibited as curiosities, but for their inherent primal beauty.

This 1950s model living room was set up in a Harlem apartment house along the Harlem River by Sachs Quality Furniture to give tenants decorating ideas. Its spare layout, as well as the furniture's boxy construction and purity of line, reflect the modernist aesthetic, and the nubby texture of fabrics and floor coverings displays its appreciation of handwoven textiles from original cultures.

The Bauhaus, too, founded by Walter Gropius in 1919 in Weimar Germany, was a catalyst for change. The International Style that was taught there and promulgated throughout the world by disciples like Moholy-Nagy and Mies van der Rohe, and by other prominent European designers such as Le Corbusier, preached a no-nonsense, form-follows-function economy, a banishment of clutter, a respect for materials, and a reductionism that approached the spiritual. Its geometry and angularity jibed perfectly with African or other ethnic accents by providing them with a pared down, elemental environment that threw their starkness and sense of spiritual power into dramatic relief. Moholy-Nagy reinvigorated traditional weaving techniques such as ikat, incorporated natural fibers, and drew upon patterns from world cultures like Africa and Japan where weaving played a central social and economic role.

Art deco and International Style were consummately urban approaches to design, popularized in cities like New York and Paris rather than in country estates or French chateaux. They embodied all that was modern—cosmopolitan sophistication, the burgeoning of industry and mass production, the coolness of jazz, the glitter of the city. They were perfect fits for Harlem Style.

The palette also changed. The new furniture designs did not look particularly elegant or modern in Victorian flowery prints. They were upholstered in natural leathers or textured earth-toned fabrics. Black, not surprisingly, took on a much more dominant role. New technologies enabled the production of tubular steel and chrome, adding the glint of silver. Animal hides, particularly zebra, leopard, and cowhide, were used with more prevalence on floors, cushions, and accent pieces such as ottomans. Bright color was employed to punctuate rooms that became almost monochromatic.

This new kind of interior décor did not immediately manifest itself across the board. The mimicking of styles popular to the old-money set was still alluring for the newly wealthy. One evening in 1926, Sir Osbert Sitwell dropped by a party at the townhouse of A'Lelia Walker, Harlem's reigning socialite. He found a marble entrance hall, gold and blue rooms, Aubusson carpets, and Louis XVI furniture. He later commented on the grand salon, "a tent room, carried out in the Parisian style of the Second Empire."

It's even fair to say that in the late 1920s and early '30s, most interiors still fell into period looks and that the dark, stuffy, over-furnished style preferred by Victorians was still the norm. Yet, a shift in thinking took place during the Harlem Renaissance. The permissiveness of its fabled nightlife and its mystique inevitably led to a relaxation of stiff, formal aesthetics and to a greater freedom in personal style. That freedom spilled into interior design in the form of a more daring approach to blending high style with low, clean modern lines with so-called "primitive" textures and artifacts, and to a wholly more organic aesthetic than what had come before.

Harlem Style spread across the country to Hollywood and leapfrogged the Atlantic to Paris and Berlin. It prefigured the work of countless interior designers. In Paris, the pioneering modernist Eileen Gray created a room with silver-leaf wallpaper and a zebra skin rug. Her early perfection of Japanese lacquering techniques and her pervasive use of animal hides to elicit a tactile, sensual response from clients whose rooms she outfitted are more easily understood in this light.

Without the liberty Harlem Style allowed, it would have been unthinkable for Elsie de Wolfe, that legendary American doyenne of French Neoclassicism, to champion a lighter, adamantly anti-Victorian palette (especially beige), or to purchase a Biedermeier-inspired Lucite chair covered in leopard. It's certainly likely that de Wolfe was exposed to the aesthetic ripples of the Harlem wave. Not only was she a prominent socialite during that era, attuned to the slightest detectable shifts in the tides of fashion, but her longtime companion was Elisabeth Marbury, a theatrical agent that Levering Lewis counts among the "Salon Negrotarians" who were fascinated with black culture and the vogue it personified at the time.

HARLEM STYLE NOW

The Harlem Renaissance receded after 1930. Succeeding decades saw periods of devastating economic decline and political upheaval. But throughout, Harlem continued to be a haven for writers, artists, musicians, and intellectuals. James Baldwin, Ralph Ellison, Romare Bearden, Jacob Lawrence, Charles White, Alberta Hunter, Louis Armstrong, Gordon Parks—the list is endless. It remains to this day a center for political discourse, having welcomed over the years figures as diverse as Malcolm X, Martin Luther King, Jr., and the Reverend Al Sharpton.

Most happily for us, Harlem has continued to be a generator of style. One need only look to the influence of black culture on music and fashion to see this is so. With reurbanization taking place on an expansive scale in America (a reurbanization Harlem began three decades ago), the freedom of style that came to typify Harlem décor after the 1920s has become popular again.

Now is the perfect moment in American history for Harlem Style. The suburb is no longer considered the idyll it was imagined to be at mid-century. Its utopian image began to crack in the post-Vietnam, post-Watergate era of the 1970s. The political movements of the '60s and '70s spurred activists to address the dilapidation and social decay of inner cities, which resulted, in the 1980s, in widespread efforts to reclaim them. Formerly neglected neighborhoods in cities across America were cleaned up, refurbished, and resettled.

To be sure, American suburbs remain robust. They are indispensable bedroom communities for ever more expensive cities, and few would dispute the theory that suburbs—with their close-knit communities, ampleness of space, and lower crime rates—are better places to rear young children.

Yet those same suburbs suffer from unchecked sprawl, making it harder to keep tabs on the children we raise there. The cookie-cutter design of many

In Roderick Shade's room for the Harlem United Showhouse in 1998, contemporary furniture, elegantly tailored slipcovers and modern paintings coexist beautifully with natural materials like grasscloth wallcoverings, a seagrass rug, and Tunisian marble mosaic tiles, as well as African sculpture.

American suburbs—with their bland conformities, their malls and fast food chains, and their dearth of cultural offerings—have also proved stifling to many. The sense of protection and security that initially drew us to suburbs has been sorely tested by events like the Columbine High School shootings. Most anything of lasting value offered by the suburbs, such as cleaner air or wide open spaces, can be found in greater abundance in the country. To many who have returned to city life, the suburb seems a kind of limbo between having it all and having only what we really, truly need.

Today, from Oakland to Providence, from Minneapolis to Dallas, inner cities are flourishing, reclaimed by people who felt creatively dead-ended in outlying suburbs. Perhaps because of New York's unique, central importance to the economic, intellectual, and cultural life of the United States, Harlem has been at the forefront of much of the reurbanization movement. Harlem sets the standard for urban spaces—the Chelsea loft, the downtown bohemian flat, or the grand townhouse. The reason is that it draws inspiration from all the stimuli present in a contemporary, multicultural metropolitan setting.

True, the terrorist attacks on the World Trade Center and the Pentagon September 11, 2001 have changed the way we think about cities, too. But this has not altered our awareness of the American suburb's limitations and has yet to result in a mass exodus from Manhattan or Washington. If anything, these events made Americans realize that building a strong sense of community has never been more important, and nowhere more so than in urban centers. The way New Yorkers handled the crisis, in fact, stands as living testament to the strength and vigor of city life and to the fortitude and humanity of its inhabitants.

The home of Evelyn and Avatar Neal on Jumel Terrace in Harlem is adorned with a comfortable, uncluttered assortment of African art, ethnic textiles, and modern and period furnishings, allowing impeccably maintained architectural details to take center stage.

HARLEM TODAY

Perhaps because of its near-mythic image, Harlem has had to protect its heart by becoming more insular than other, less fabled communities. It's not surprising or unwarranted. White attendance at black society gatherings in Harlem thinned out with the arrival of the Great Depression, and once Prohibition was repealed, those who had come seeking "low-down" entertainments stopped taking the A train going north. There was a sense of betrayal, a shuttering, a closing of doors. And, says Reverend Butts, pastor of Abyssinian Baptist Church on West 138th Street, "Since the death of Adam Powell, no one paid much attention to Harlem. It had been ignored."

The generation that remembers earlier days is a little gun shy, not unjustly, about being exploited again in some way. "The old-timers have a desirable smugness," explains Reverend Butts. "But you need that—you need someone to be able to say, 'I remember the funeral of Bill Bojangles Robinson. I remember the parades of Marcus Garvey.' You appreciate those historical characters in the community," he says, even if "some are wary."

These late nineteenth-century row houses lining the cobblestone streets of Sylvan Terrace—across from the Morris-Jumel Mansion where George Washington actually did sleep—are among the few remaining examples of wood-frame structures built in the post-Revolutionary War period.

For there is another renaissance blooming in Harlem today. This time, the flood is not just white and rich, but of all colors and from all economic strata. "Business has increased because residential opportunities have increased," says Rev. Butts, himself a Harlem resident of more than thirty years. "It's not all poor people. You have a large population of middle class and, with the restoration of business, an upper class. And with that has come the need for services—shoe stores, a Disney store, health food shops, sports clubs, a kite shop."

Harlem properties are among the hottest real estate in Manhattan. Prices have soared and lower-income residents fear being gentrified right out of the old neighborhood. Whole blocks of houses that had become neglected single-room occupancy hotels require considerable funds to refurbish, funds that seem increasingly to flow from younger hands that crave the feel of PalmPilots and Range Rovers but have little memory of what made Harlem such a vibrant center some seventy-five years ago. Longtime residents, says Rev. Butts, feel "moved in on" and are afraid the neighborhood will lose its character.

"All of us, not only in Harlem, have to be concerned about affordable housing in New York," he explains. "We all have to be vigilant. But you can't develop a community, improve its services and sanitation, if you only have poor people living in it. You need a mixture of incomes." Butts agrees that there will always be trendsetters who descend on a place while it is popular and disappear just as quickly when it begins to lose its luster or sense of novelty. To some extent, Van Vechten and his circle was such a group. But it was also one of the catalysts of the Harlem Renaissance. "I don't know how you police that," Rev. Butts says. "Carl Van Vechten and all of them were part of the community. It was what it was. I don't know how you avoid those patrons who come to exploit. Besides, in that exploitation is the revelation of art. You know, people criticized Elvis Presley for stealing black music. 'Hound Dog' wasn't his song, but because of him it got out there. History sort of takes its course."

Peggy Scott-Hammond's Hamilton Terrace home is a good example of the preservationist approach to Harlem renovations, which seeks to restore details like moldings and leaded glass to their original condition. Yet her blend of global artifacts with more Eurocentric pieces (a classical garden planter, candlesticks, and Limoges) exhibits a contemporary feel for design.

In some very good ways, the current renaissance parallels the original. Today, there are many artists and writers living in Harlem, U.S.A., as its proud residents refer to their historic portion of Manhattan Island. Brett Cook-Dizney has made a name for himself with portraits of ordinary Harlem residents he memorializes as local heroes by depicting them in larger-than-life outdoor murals. Maya Angelou has purchased property here. Galleries abound and fine restaurants have sprung up in every quarter, serving up a whole world of cuisines, from traditional Southern to the most nouvelle of the nouvelle.

There is a large gay population, most of which is more open than the homosexual writers and intellectuals of the 1920s and '30s who frequented the drag balls at the Manhattan Casino/Rockland Palace (280 West 155th Street) and Edmond's Cellar (2161 Fifth Avenue). The sense of "demimonde" still exists, however, in groups like the Third Rail, a gathering of black gay men who enjoy thug culture, duds, and attitude and meet by invitation and word-of-mouth at roving locations around Harlem.

Harlem is still a community with a very strong sense of itself, with a distinct and identifiable personality unlike any other neighborhood in New York. "To keep the flavor of Harlem as an African-American community and to make sure poor people don't get kicked out, people have had to be active, keep the battle cry going," says Rev. Butts. "Hard times, if nothing else, will organize people." Continuing that sort of activism can ensure the area's character is preserved. "The flavor of the community as a hotbed for African-American activity will always remain. That's something that people from around the world come here to enjoy."

In this book, you will see how many of Harlem's denizens live. Not all of them have appointed their apartments or brownstones in the contemporary Harlem Style on which we concentrate here. There are those who are strongly preservationist and prefer to live in the high Victorian splendor that typified the area prior at the turn of the last century.

Harlem Style has not been transplanted intact from the era following the Harlem Renaissance into this one. Rather, it has evolved and grown, absorbing newer styles into its overall global view. But its mixture of natural and industrial materials, of high and low style, of organic and slick textures, of urbane comfort balanced with a hip edge, and its dependence on a largely monochromatic, earth-bound palette—in short, all the basic precepts of Harlem Style that originated just before mid-century—continue to inform the work of many interior designers today.

We've also included several interiors that break completely out of any identifiable style—six "Harlem Originals" scattered throughout the book—and, in so doing, bring to Harlem a most particular flavor you're unlikely to encounter anywhere else—a quaint cottage interior that seems lifted from the coast of Maine and transported to a Harlem brownstone, an old Stanford White home on Strivers' Row whose parlor has been transformed into an enormous shrine to various Indian swamis, a den that houses a collection of American Indian art and artifacts you'd more readily expect to see in Santa Fe or San Antonio. For even though these may appear to be anomalies, the truth is that they, too, represent a facet of Harlem Style because they spring from the same liberality of spirit that has always characterized life here.

This is our ode to the incredible diversity that is Harlem Style.

elements of harlem style

What we call Harlem Style has been referred to variously as "urban," "Manhattan" and "global." Yet Harlem Style is all of these things and none in particular. The word urban today is practically synonymous with hip hop or gangsta rap edginess and brings to mind poured concrete floors, exposed steel beams, and graffiti. "Manhattan" is a more serviceable term, yet implies a kind of Park Avenue chic—lots of Biedermeier or Louis, bronze gilding, and highly polished surfaces. And "global" references an aesthetic that is so-called "Third World," quaintly handcrafted and anti-industrial. All of these ideas and aesthetics have contributed to Harlem Style, yet none pervades it absolutely.

There are no hard and fast rules in Harlem Style. Almost anything goes, as long as the result has purpose and a kind of understated flair. To better understand how it all comes together, it's useful to parse the style into various elements, which can then be freely mixed in infinite combinations to achieve this end. There are two overarching principles however: The aesthetics of Harlem Style depend largely on the interplay between the rough-hewn and the refined, between purely sensory response and a nuanced, sophisticated discourse—and a sense of glamour always elevates the quotidian.

LEFT: **Roderick Shade's design for the Harlem United Showhouse brings together various elements of Harlem Style—use of simple form, ethnic influences, and textural contrasts.** PREVIOUS PAGE: **The Philadelphia living room of Kevin Burns and Igor Rivlin, owners of USONA Home Furnishings.**

MONOCHROMATICS AND THE PLAY OF LIGHT

Listen to three designers, whose work we feature, discuss color.

JOHN BARMAN "Colors seem more natural to an environment when you bring the colors that are outdoors in. In the country you have greens. In the city, when you look out the window you see more neutral colors—gray, brick, brownstone. So I use neutrals with bright colors as accents, unless a client is particularly in love with color."

RICHARD MISHAAN "This isn't carved in stone, but, basically, color can be used as long as it's subdued. For example, instead of bright yellow, maize; greens are usually more sage or celadon; blues are light, powdery. They're hues really, not colors, and they're all taken from nature."

MARIO ARANDA "I use natural colors, yes. But the sky gets really blue, the grass gets really electric green, and geraniums can be a pretty audacious pink. You see so much concrete and so much brown and gray—washed-out stuff—that I look for the antidote to that."

Light becomes the transformative force in a monochromatic setting by Dallas designer Gary Jackson for Jackson Ivey-Jackson Interior.

These would seem to be three contradictory ways of coming at one subject, yet in the context of Harlem Style, they all have suitable applications. Color is a complex and emotional thing; one client may adore Chinese red while another wouldn't think of being surrounded by anything but linen white walls. So throughout this book, the use of color will traverse a wide spectrum. Yet if you flip these pages quickly, you would probably come to some basic conclusions about the way Harlem Style sees color.

THE MONOCHROMATIC PALETTE

Harlem Style is predicated largely on an earthy, nearly monochromatic palette. Color functions as a kind of neutral stage set or, in Darryl Carter's words, "like a blank canvas" for showcasing other elements of Harlem Style such as interesting furniture or artifacts. It is hardly ever the main attraction and rarely the first thing a person notices in the room. A wall or alcove may be rendered in a strong, eye-grabbing shade, but the use of this effect is usually decorative and occasional rather than all-encompassing.

Earth tones are pervasive. Taupe, beige, all manner of brown from fawn to chocolate, and clay or brick shades are reminiscent of the genre's African origins. They bring warmth to a room that is indispensable for Harlem Style. And they add the all-important element of nature, specifically an association with the great variety of Africa's soils—from the arid sands of the Sahara, to the fertile black loam of the Congo's rainforest, to the red-tinted clay of the Namibian steppe.

This natural, soothing monochrome also brings a balancing calm to a room. "Most of the people who come to me have high-power city jobs," says Eve Robinson. "I try to create sophisticated interiors that are also places to relax by using very soft backgrounds, lots of taupes and creams. The strong color is on pillows or other accents. This creates a sense of sereneness."

MONOCHROMATIC

Aside from imparting a sense of calm, the monochromatic palette serves to bring other details of a room to the fore. PREVIOUS PAGE: **In Darryl Carter's Washington, D.C. living room, the color scheme allows for greater appreciation of subtle lines (the curves** on the fire-place mantel and sofas), art, and ethnic elements like the Indonesian drum table. ABOVE: **Ivory walls are a subtle backdrop for the sensual textures of dark wood, leather, and fur in a display at USONA Home Furnishings in Philadelphia.** RIGHT: **A warm eggshell color and whitewashed wood floors serve to highlight the elegant line of the ceiling and fireplace, a dramatic elephant tusk, and a 1950s metal sunburst wall sculpture in Marc Anderson's East Harlem bedroom.**

Harlem Originals

"I am a memory woman," says Harlem real estate agent Lana Turner, "someone who has extreme reverence for things that are old but still resonate with the present."

This much seems clear as you tour Turner's rambling apartment on the top floor of a ten-story, circa 1916 building at 141st Street and Convent Avenue. A Victorian-style sofa and two overstuffed armchairs are upholstered in a grandmotherly rose-colored brocade. There is a glass-fronted, demi-lune china cabinet with gold trim filled with old-fashioned porcelain patterns. A lampshade, with its scalloped edge and six-inch fringe, looks plucked from the 1920s or '30s. There's no doubt you sense Old Harlem in these rooms.

What is less apparent is how the apartment—its composition and decoration—actually mirrors the process of memory. Memory is a chimera; intangible, fleeting, and not entirely reliable. What it retains is really the idea of something, rather than the thing itself. And ideas are fluid. They swim into each other, making it impossible to separate the brackish waters of one from the fresh water of another. Even if we think we succeed in parsing them into components, something from one memory, some miniscule drop, lingers inextricably in another, coloring it ever so slightly, yet irrevocably.

So Turner is attracted to objects that evoke the concepts of things. The painting over the sofa of what looks like a jazz musician, for example, is actually a fiction. It is by a white artist from Syracuse who himself plays the blues, yet the man in the painting is not a real person. Still, somehow, he looks familiar. "He makes me think about my uncles, the men I see on Saturday nights, the men at church," observes Turner. And though this man holds no instrument (unless there's a harmonica we can't see in the pockets where he's tucked his hands) the sound of the blues emanates silently from the picture.

That is precisely what Turner is after. Blues, she says, "is very funny in its sadness. It's like a good story. Embedded within simple lines are the lives of people who might seem hopeless, but the music turns it around in a way you can hear and tells you this is also a moment to celebrate." This painting is all of those things: sad, funny, painful, comforting, ripe with soul—and music.

There are also black dolls, folk art, and rustic crosses collected on trips to Santa Fe, where, says Turner, "I go with clockwork

THE REALTOR

regularity to see the sky." One piece she particularly likes is a sculpture called *Those Who Have Gone on Before* of two back-to-back figures. Around their waists are strings hung with pencils, buttons, beads, caps, charms. The specific memories these objects relate to are a mystery to everyone but the artist, yet Turner says she can project onto it her own memories, add her own symbols to layer it with personal meaning.

Turner would never describe herself as a realtor. Though she makes a living selling properties and buildings, her life, like ideas, is fluid. She is project director for the African-American Burial Ground in lower Manhattan and produces a section on minority business for *Fortune* magazine. She also chairs a women's literary society with almost 100 members, small groups of which gather regularly in her home to discuss books and poetry. Which means there are many, many books. Except for family photos along a sliver of wall—more memories—books line an entire room almost completely from floor to ceiling. And these, of course, represent still other memories; personal memories of the authors spun into works of art that become different kinds of memories in the lives of those who read them.

THE REALTOR

BLACK AND WHITE

This coupling is perhaps the most direct link to Harlem Style's roots in the Jazz Age. Think of any movie you've seen or book you've read on the era. What invariably springs to mind is an ubiquity of black-and-white checkered dance floors and the drawings of jazz musicians and dancers limned by artists like Miguel Covarrubias and Al Hirshfeld. It was a color scheme that expressed the boldness and forthrightness of the time. It embodied the minimalist aesthetic approach of movements like *l'esprit nouveau* and the Bauhaus. And it also carried racial metaphors that could be perceived positively (like blacks and whites co-existing).

The black-and-white colorway also possesses obvious connections to quintessentially African materials: ebony, bone, and ivory. Its infinite gradations—from inky flatness to obsidian luminosity, from porcelain white to tones tinted with hints of blue, yellow, or pink—afford it a versatility of application unequalled by any other combination of hues. Within the vernacular of Harlem Style, the starkness of black and white is usually tempered with a mix of organic and subtle shades. They are never used exclusively, as this would produce environments that are sterile, emotionally blank, and at odds with the aims of Harlem Style to create natural, personalized settings that have nuance and dimension.

In their Harlem living room, architect William Ryall and Columbia University professor of architectural history Barry Bergdoll created a study in black and white.

The tendency for starkness in this combination is relieved by a red lacquered coffee table and the tactile textures of brick and coarse-weave fabrics.

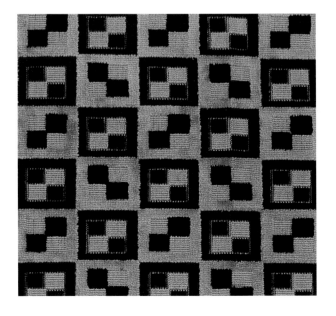

The austerity of the black-and-white scheme is counteracted by, ABOVE, rich, polished wood grain on floor and furnishings in John Barman's bedroom and, OPPOSITE, by the distressed metal surface of the old bar that serves as Harlem floral designer Marc Wilson's bedside table, its wrought-iron base, and the introduction of wheat grass. LEFT: Fabric by Kravet recalls the mosaic tile floors of the 1930s and '40s.

METALLICS

A whole range of metallic shades is incorporated through-out Harlem Style interiors. "Metallics were popular in the 1920s, '30s, and '40s, then they disappeared," observes John Barman. "Now they're acceptable again."

Different designers utilize metallics is varying ways. Some, like Barman, exploit their shine to achieve a sense of glamour. "Glamour is important in the city," he says, "and shinier metals and crystal convey this. That's the image you have of Harlem and New York in the 1920s and '30s."

Barman also points out that metallics reflect light, which is too often fleeting in the city, dulled by smog or ducking furtively behind a high-rise. As Tony Whitfield puts it, "Light in contemporary environments plays an enormously important role, and the colors that are used are those that allow light to become a factor, that take on new characteristics in various kinds of light." Even though he is speaking gener-ally here of color, it's clear that metallics are most sensitive to light's caprices. There is no more immediate or palpable way to accomplish the objective of capturing and transforming light's mutability than by using metallics to reflect and transform it.

Other designers use metallics to impart texture and a feeling of faded grandeur. Darryl Carter, for instance, often dips brass fixtures in acid "to take away their shine and make them look more bronze." Mario Aranda likes to use "pocked and irregular brass, materials that are closer to their origins." Which is to say materials, and metallics in particular, in their most raw and unfinished state, prior to the buffing, burnishing, or "refining" of human hands.

This approach has its practical aspects, too. For Clodagh, it's a question of maintenance, as well as a metaphysical concern. "Texture gives a sense of permanence," she believes. "I grew up in a Georgian house in Ireland where every

In this room by Clodagh, various metals are exploited for both their reflective quality and, through various distressing techniques, their textural richness. The latter lends a comforting feeling of permanence to what are normally hard, cold materials.

morning you'd come downstairs and someone was polishing silver. You knew the shine was impermanent. The urban environment makes you very aware of your time poverty. So, unless you're into the Zen of silver polishing, who needs it? You don't want to come home to an apartment that's going to wave its finger at you and say, 'Maintain me, maintain me!'"

METALLICS

Whether highly polished or distressed by brushing, sanding, and acid-streaking, metallics are one of the most effective tools for capturing and transforming light and color. LEFT: The deep blue-purple-pink palette and the light bouncing off glass and Lucite objects in this room by Christopher Coleman are both absorbed into and reflected by the brushed steel chest of drawers. RIGHT: Clockwise from top left, patinated and sculpted tile inserts and trim from Ann Sacks; Hammered Silver and Hammered Gold wallpapers from Donghia Furniture/Textiles Ltd.; and stainless steel mosaic tile from Ann Sacks.

STRONG COLOR ACCENTS

The ability of color to influence mood has been exhaustively documented. There is amazing dramatic potential in the use of strong color. And the flipside of what has been pejoratively called modernism's "beige and greige" tendency is the risk that monochrome will become just plain monotone.

Strong color is extremely useful as a tool for personalizing space. It can also bring humor and youthful freshness to an interior. For example, in speaking of neutrals, Christopher Coleman says, "I try talking people out of white. And if you use white, use five or six shades of white; play with it to create mood and drama. You're only young once. You might as well have fun now."

Clodagh often uses strong color whimsically, too, by placing it in unexpected, out-of-sight locations such as closets and pantries. "It's to do with being unpredictable," she explains, "like flashing your underwear."

Color can also enhance the global feel of an urban space. "The way we work with color seems invariably to have an ethnic reference," observes Clodagh. "We talk about Burmese red or a mud cloth amber."

In Sharne Algotsson's Philadelphia morning room, which she calls "mood indigo," the blue wall is a tribute to the most commonly used natural dye in Africa, while gold cross-hatch lines symbolize the continent's western gold coast. Together they add warmth and depth and provide a vibrant contrast for an eclectic mix of patterns and textiles.

Color can enliven simple architecture and furnishings or enhance more ornate ones. RIGHT: **John Barman** uses a bright, Morrocan-style yellow-and-red fabric to punch up the fun factor in this space and to reflect the ethnic feel of pieces like the Indian bed that serves as his coffee table. OPPOSITE: **Richard Mishaan** brings flair to blocky, clean-lined mono-chromatic furniture by using a yellow-tinted green on the walls, then adds a sense of fun with fur-covered ottomans on antler-like iron legs at Homer, his store on Madison Avenue.

Among the shades commonly showcased in these rooms are specifically ethnic ones like China red or Indian turquoise, pastels like lavender and pink, spice shades such as saffron and paprika, bold greens like chartreuse, or more acid variations that hint toward yellow, pale ice blue, and chocolate brown. Really, though, any color that you are fond of blends well with the monochromatic "canvas" of Harlem Style as long as it is used judiciously. The object, once again, is to provide contrasts that are interesting or unexpected.

Harlem Originals

The front parlor of Dr. Barbara Ann Teer's brownstone on 137th Street is redolent with incense. The even, incessant sounds of chanting emanate from an audio system that sits on the parquet floor.

Pictures of Swami Muktananda and his disciple, Gurumayi, are propped against candles, stones, African figures, and drums, forming a makeshift altar in front of an ornately carved nineteenth-century mantel. Offerings of corn, flowers, potted plants, and gourds are everywhere.

Dr. Teer came to New York to be in the theater, before helping found the Negro Ensemble Company with Robert Hooks, Douglas Turner Ward, and Gerald Krone. During the Civil Rights Movement, she was encouraged by her activist sister, Frederica L. Teer, to create a theater of "revival and ritual" that "addressed the creative concerns of people of African descent." In 1968, Dr. Teer established the National Black Theatre (today the National Black Theatre's Institute of Action Arts) to produce original experimental performance works. Part of the National Black Theatre experience incorporated a system of meditation devised by Dr. Teer that adopted many of the same principles as other non-Western devotions, including Yoruba religions, Hawaiian healing practices and Haitian systems.

All the spiritual methodologies she has studied have a basic philosophy shared by all Africans. "African people view the world from the inside," she explains, "not the outside, which is ego-based. My job is to build an institution that uses energy rightly, because all there is is energy."

Over the years, Dr. Teer became involved with Siddha, one of the nine yogas. Twice a week, she has friends come over to chant before the altar. "The key to healing humanity is right here in Harlem," she believes. "We are the original people, the parent people of the planet. We had civilization long before there was ever a conversation about Europe." Dr. Teer's unshakable certainty in this belief manifests itself in a space that is crammed with African art, and furniture covered in mud cloth, hides, and African fabrics.

So why would the key to healing humanity be in Harlem and not in Africa? "Because we as a people, being brought forcefully to this country, blended the best of the Eastern and Western systems." The key, says Dr. Teer, "lies in finding the blend."

THE TRANSCENDENTALIST

STRONG COLOR

Strong color is one of the most effective ways to personalize a space. LEFT: Chicago designer Mario Aranda warms a high-ceilinged open space with bright green and red walls that also play off rugs and textiles. TOP RIGHT: In Peggy Scott-Hammond's Harlem home, color is used to evoke global influences, particularly North African or Indian. BOTTOM RIGHT: In Ron Melichar's Hamilton Heights living room, a strong gray-green and mustard-gold set off the richness of wood and tile details and provide a backdrop for furniture from the West and Far East, Rookwood and Van Briggle art pottery, and Japanese woodblock prints above the mantelpiece.

STRONG COLOR

ABOVE: **At Homer, Richard Mishaan's Madison Avenue design store, his use of lilac-tinted blue on a wall makes white furniture and pottery pop out at the viewer, whereas they would almost disappear against a more neutral background shade.**

RIGHT: **The visual impact of a red wall in the hallway speaks for itself, but in this apartment, designed by Marc Anderson, it also creates a color dialogue with the Chinese wedding cabinet that holds pride of place in the living room.**

Clodagh uses color as an
element of surprise, "like
flashing your underwear."
Here, a translucent purple
door is the only vibrant
hue in an otherwise sub-
dued and earthy setting.

A STUDY IN CONTRASTS

One of the chief concerns of any decorative style is to create rooms that are distinctive. Each age has its particular device for achieving this. For the Europeans of the baroque era, it was a surfeit of gilding and a reliance on curvaceous, feminine forms. For the Arts & Crafts movement, it was a return to the austere purity of Gothic styles and the nobility of craftsmanship. For deco, the pairing of simple, "primitive" form with bold, graphic line represented what was *au courant*.

One of Harlem Style's most distinctive devices is its blending of textures. Again, here are a few designers discussing the same topic. This time, what is striking is how much they echo the same powerful sentiment.

CLODAGH "I design an experience more than a space...Things have to be very tactile."
MARIO ARANDA "People are generally afraid of their senses. But I always look for a very corporal, sensual response with textures and deep colors."
YOLANDA FERRELL-BROWN "I like people to have a very sensory experience in the rooms they live in. That's part of the layering of texture and detail. You discover more the more time you spend there."

Texture enhances our tactile response to an environment. In Kevin Burns and Igor Rivlin's Philadelphia bedroom, matte textures play off shiny ones and the controlled basket weave of the leather bed plays against the thick, helter-skelter pile of a musk-ox fur rug.

TONY WHITFIELD "Textures and textiles are very important in environments because they are evocative. [In Harlem Style] you find a play of textures that includes everything from banana fibers to hemps to silks to suedes. There are more subtle combinations of materials, and new ways of processing fibers that go beyond the nubby tweed of the 1960s and the shag rug. Texture, in general, is more complex."

Perhaps for all designers working in a contemporary urban idiom, texture is the place where they like to experiment most. Unlike previous decorative genres however, where texture is concerned, the emphasis is not on the aspirational. It is in the sphere where the coarse and the soft co-exist, where plebian mingles with luxurious, that these designers, and Harlem Style, like to dwell. "The use of materials is totally different," says Richard Mishaan. "Mixes that create a contrast or tension are what define urban style."

There are practical reasons for this as well. Busy urban living places a much higher priority on easy maintenance and, says Clodagh, "textured surfaces reflect light and imperfections more kindly."

But most of all, it is a means to an end—the end being, of course, to create a room that provides subtle stimulation; stimulation that works on the senses in an untaxing, practically imperceptible, way.

As with many of these designers, Yolanda Ferrell-Brown likes to approach texture as a weight issue. She says: "Mohair has a weight to it. And how does that look next to silk or velvet? The high sheen with the matte? Linen is light and opalescent. It's the juxtaposition of different materials that is more contemporary."

The array of textures used in Harlem Style runs the gamut from coarse to highly finished, from hard and opaque to soft and gossamer. This textural mix reaches into every facet of home design. It is used in fabrics, of course, but also wall treatments and flooring. The jazz metaphor of "call and response" is useful here (or, for that matter, in any of the individual elements covered in this chapter). Think of two instruments with different sounds and tonal qualities carrying on a musical dialogue—the silkiness of a

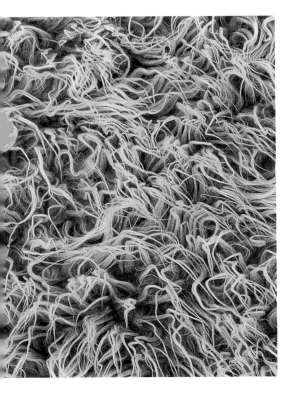

PREVIOUS PAGE: **Fashion designer Edward Wilkerson's bedroom is a symphony of sensual textures: smooth-planed wood on the bed next to rougher, notch-carved wood on the African spider web table, coarsely woven natural fibers on the rug and finer woven ones on the large lidded basket, and cool white linen paired with warm fur.** LEFT: **Some textures just demand to be touched: clockwise from top left, faux fur by Kravet, an intricate appliqué look on kuba cloth from South Africa, Tunisian mosaic tiles from Artistic Tile on a fireplace surround designed by Roderick Shade, and woven silk by Kravet.**

tenor sax or the reediness of a clarinet, say, contrasted by the brassy blare of a trumpet. The one answers and highlights the other.

Where fabrics are concerned, heavy woven textiles such as mud cloth or kuba cloth mix comfortably with silkier iridescent textiles like taffeta. Furs (real or faux) pair off with patent leather or vinyl, or with jacquards and velvets. Bouclé couples with rubberized finishes or polyurethaned fabrics.

Treatments for wall and floor are similarly diverse and create an animated dialogue between the hand-wrought and the commercially produced. Organic textures temper cool industrial ones. In the organic camp are grass cloths, silk papers, handmade papers flecked with natural elements, tumbled stone, cork and leather tiles, and vinyl wall coverings that have been textured to resemble something more woven or grass-like. Unpapered walls tend to recall the feel of sand or the look of mottled Venetian plaster. They are made of split-faced marble, covered with mosaics or flame-finished.

In the industrial-materials camp there are wall partitions and doors made of glass that has been electrochromed, frosted, or sandblasted. There is pewter, stainless steel, nickel, bronze and white bronze, and a host of other metals. Most commonly, the finishes are gentle—brushed or satin versus shiny—and many boast matte or textured treatments like those achieved through distressing, oxidizing, hammering, and acid-streaking.

And, says Christopher Coleman, "I'm big on wallpaper. Young people have such a fear of wallpaper. But it's half the time and money of paint, and there's so much more available: rubbed metallics, cork, and ground papers that look like lacquer."

Harlem Originals

If you're feeling like Harlem Style is looking a little pale and wan, a visit to Cary Liebowitz in Hamilton Heights is our recommended palliative. You don't really have to have been a Grateful Dead fan or dropped acid to appreciate what Liebowitz has done in this turn-of-the-century home... but it helps.

Liebowitz is a print specialist at Christie's auction house. He's also a major shopper. In a way, this proclivity led him to Harlem. Born in Manhattan and raised in Connecticut, he had been living in Brooklyn for some time and had managed to acquire an enormous amount of curiosities and a contemporary art collection that simply did not fit into his Carroll Gardens digs. "I wanted a lot more wall space," he recalls. Liebowitz looked all over Manhattan, but felt "the karma wasn't right for most places."

His karma improved at the upper reaches of St. Nicholas Avenue. The block between 152nd and 153rd Street had been designed by one architect, Clarence True, in the 1890s. "It was a middle class, bourgeois sort of residence," explains Liebowitz of his purchase. "It had more of a townhouse lay-out than a brownstone with a stoop." It also had lots of wall space, a challenge for less acquisitive souls, but an open invitation to people like Liebowitz.

The lexicon of interior design does not possess a neat, tidy term that accurately describes Liebowitz's highly personal approach to decoration. Insolent and insurgent, however, seem appropriate words to define the basic impulse from which he operates. It's not just the Pee Wee's Playhouse palette of pink, red, orange, purplish blue, and white. It's not even the various components of a room when considered by themselves. It's the way Liebowitz combines things that turns our cozy ideas about design on their overly cultivated ear.

Consider the fabric he picked up at a flea market years ago boasting repeating red line-drawings of the Black Panthers' defiantly raised fist. It had not been fully colored in or cut properly from the bolts at the textile factory, but no matter. Liebowitz stashed it away for later use.

THE APPRAISER

When he moved to Harlem, the fabric took on a whole new meaning. Yet Liebowitz wasn't content to upholster just any piece of furniture with this symbol of black rebellion. Instead, he bought some "really fake looking Louis furniture"—a style exemplifying white European bourgeois taste, yet made ideologically suspect by the garish nature of its reproduction—and covered it with the Black Panther fists. This tongue-in-cheek challenge to white supremacy is combined with psychedelic pink wallpaper, a poofy lambs-wool tuffet and an obsessively stitched, primordial-looking chair. Regardless of season, Santa Claus and a white Teddy bear smile innocently from the faux Louis settee, oblivious to the enormous painting of a crotch, its ambiguous sex concealed behind equally androgynous underwear, standing behind them.

Acid anyone?

THE APPRAISER

CULTURE, GEOMETRICS, AND MID-CENTURY REDUX

A marriage of solids and patterns is also essential. But the patterns we're talking about here have nothing to do with flowers or toile de Jouy, both of which are more at home in a country cottage than a city high-rise. The easiest way to determine what patterns are more apt for Harlem Style is to think, again, about what city living represents. Think about business and, especially, the advertising milieu, which in urban settings seem increasingly distilled into two extremes. To navigate these worlds, you must have an appreciation of subtlety in manner, while you must equally depend on a degree of brash honesty, with a point that must be made in a sound byte and little time to waste on nuance. It's a persistent give-and-take of subliminal verbiage and bold statement, of delicate insinuation as well as out-and-out arm-twisting. And, of course, these worlds are also irrevocably multicultural nowadays, which means they are comprised of many races, traditions, and customs.

In Edward Wilkerson's living room, a riot of geometric patterns on carpets creates tension between the assertively styled shapes of African and Chinese furniture and the softness of fur pillows and a fur rug.

PATTERN

LEFT: A dining room display at Mosaic Antique and Contemporary Design, Aline Matsika's New York store. Matsika is an avid collector of African fabrics. Here, the stars are various patterns unified by color scheme— on vertical African textile panels, an African-inspired rug design, and ottomans upholstered alternately with stripes, solid color, and a contemporary fabric dotted with African symbols. RIGHT: four African-inspired fabrics, one from Donghia Furniture/ Textiles Ltd. (shown top right), and three from Kravet. FOLLOWING PAGE: In this room by Christopher Coleman, a subtle color palette comes alive against a stenciled checker pattern on the wall that takes its cue from the larger checks of the cabinet.

With these ideas in mind, some examples of the types of patterns that fit well into Harlem Style are:

ETHNICALLY-INSPIRED DESIGNS especially zigzags, repeating X shapes, and undulating, wavy lines. "We scan a lot of basket weaving to make fabrics, carpets and rug patterns," says Clodagh. "And we use ethnic weavings a lot."

ANIMAL HIDES particularly the highly graphic patterns of zebra, leopard, and cowhide. "Animal prints are great," enthuses John Barman. "They work with everything. It's the one thing that made it through completely from the 1920s and '30s to today. There's drama to them."

STRIPES thick, broad ones as opposed to thin and delicate.

PRINTS OF REPEATING MINISCULE PATTERN those that recall Secessionist Viennese textiles, for example. Minute cross-hatch patterns, subtly duo-toned twills, and herringbone weaves. Short lines and small dots randomly strewn across a fabric surface, such as those of the 1950s.

GEOMETRICS either the bold examples of tribal symbology or retro, Jetson-style. Says Eve Robinson, "I use geometric patterns, subtly, to create a sense of order," like repeating a grid around a room and executing it in different materials or colors on a floor and wall. Graphic tile patterns on floors and walls create drama too, especially when they are bold (alternating 24-inch tiles or tiles laid in stripe or zigzag patterns).

It's not always necessary spend a $150 a yard on fabric or lay down an intricately patterned carpet to get the design element you need. Many times, explains Christopher Coleman, you can use "common materials in unusual ways—plastic laminates in the bathroom, garment lining sewn into square or diamond patterns for curtains, carpet remnants sewn together into patterns on the floor."

LEFT: **All sorts of patterns work well in Harlem Style: clockwise from top left, bold geometrics in the triangle weave of a wool rug by Patterson, Flynn & Martin; North African-inspired designs on tiles by Ann Sacks; a two-tone, striped-weave rug from Patterson, Flynn & Martin; and a freestyle tile design by a Nigerian artist in the Harlem sun room of Barbara Ann Teer's brownstone.**
RIGHT: **On 122nd Street, Rod Keenan elegantly pairs a geometric grid painting of squares in alternating hues against horizontally striped fabric on tapered-back dining chairs.**

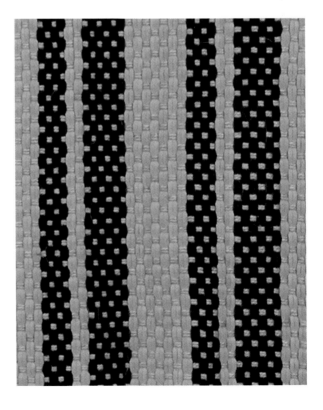

BARE IS BEAUTIFUL

This wall at Mario Aranda's
loft in an old shirt factory in
Chicago echoes the build-
ing's industrial past. Aranda
repaired it only in parts
where the plaster was
crumbling, then simply left
it bare. The result is both
lovely and dramatic.

Modern living is nothing if not more open—freer about sex, less concerned with veiling emotions, and confessional in literature, politics, and public life. We are in an age of fluid sexuality, of memoirs, of televised mea culpas. This was bound to have an effect on interiors as well. Gone are the formal, rigidly composed spaces of the Victorians. Where Harlem Style is concerned, think of the exposed brick of the speakeasy, the poured concrete of the Bauhaus and the skeletal steel girding of skyscrapers. Part of its accessibility lies in its interest in interior life as opposed to burnished façade; it seeks out the structure and inner workings of things rather than hiding them. Beautifully varnished surfaces are far from taboo, but they are only part of the whole amalgam.

Designers have left no material unexamined, and found beauty in what was formerly considered common, crude or even ugly. "Showing the bare bones of a building is something we got into the 1970s," says Tony Whitfield. "We still have it, but there's a tendency now to be selective about what is exposed. It's dealt with as texture and detail, as opposed to rawness."

As glamorous as John Barman's interiors can be, he finds a certain honesty in industrial materials that is more peculiar to city life. Like looking out the window and seeing the city's structures in all their monochromatic variations, he sizes up urban interiors with equal scrutiny. "I live with concrete floors. I like to see the city the way it is," he avers.

This is not just a New York, or Harlem phenomenon. It is a condition of city life. In Chicago, for instance, Mario Aranda lives in an old shirt factory built in 1908 by Polish and Czech immigrants. "I resist the tendency to erase that past," he says. "The wall was crumbling, so I repaired the parts of the plaster that were badly damaged and left the wall as it was, without painting it. People come from an office or a subway car and want something that reflects character, warmth, or patina."

EXPOSED CONSTRUCTION

Floral designer Marc Wilson lives in a converted Harlem schoolhouse. The floor, worn and scuffed by generations of elementary age children, was left as is, creating a kind of "exposed" construction that harks back to the building's former life and also adds texture to the room.

LEFT AND OPPOSITE: **At the
Harlem home of William
Ryall and Barry Bergdoll,
exposed brick, undisguised
floor joists, and a skeletal
stair give the interior spaces
an open and honest feel, and
also add tactile character.**

The skeleton of a room operates much as the monochromatic palette in
Harlem Style—as a canvas or stage set. Each designer examines that skeleton as
his or her jumping-off point, making judgments about its value and appeal in
the general scheme of décor. That doesn't mean structure is always desirable, just
that it is not necessarily unattractive. "If you had a room that was weaker in
architectural value," says Richard Mishaan, "you'd paint it red or some Billy
Baldwin color. But in contemporary urban design, bringing out the architectural
structure in a home really serves as a way to set a tone for the artwork, furniture,
everything...Things are less hidden, less transformed."

Harlem Originals

There's no getting away from Brett Cook-Dizney in his live-work space on 127th Street—whether he's there alongside you or not. Even if Cook-Dizney isn't corporally present, his likeness is everywhere, repeatedly limned on a larger-than-life scale from one end of this loft to the other.

Like Rembrandt, an artist with whom Cook-Dizney shares the same penchant for obsessive self-analysis worked out in paint and pencil, he is his most constant subject.

There's Cook-Dizney's face, enormously behind the bed, by the stove, visible in three Technicolor versions from the table where he eats. His visage is in the painting studio, which is sealed off from the rest of the space by heavy metal doors and elaborately ventilated to disperse the fumes of his art. He's there in the gallery area—as a geeky, outsized pubescent with his prom date and as a bare-chested adult with flowing dreadlocks looking down at you provocatively.

Technically, Cook-Dizney is an aerosol artist. Spray paints are his materials. They are by definition commercial, by default unsubtle and lacking in versatility of tone or value. You can't dilute them, can't mix them to create more nuanced shades. He achieves his amazingly broad palette of gradations by multiple layerings of like colors, or by affecting the tonal quality of an area by surrounding it with a contrasting tone.

The spare furnishings of his loft exhibit similar qualities: the colors are bright and saturated—purple, burnt orange, blue—and the style commercial in the manner of La-Z-Boy recliners and early, industrially produced office furniture. Yet their generic qualities are relieved by what is around them, specifically the hard-working, worn warmth of exposed brick and a stunning variegated display of spider plants.

Cook-Dizney is extremely smart. He's talented, charming, gregarious, and good-looking. Some would even say he is successful. He has good reason to be a self-indulgent, self-aggrandizing bully à la Pollack or Warhol. Yet he's not—at all.

To be sure, Cook-Dizney is no fool. He is deeply aware of his talents. He knows he has brought the Rembrandtesque visual

THE ARTIST

memoir into the present. He's done it by using the defining medium of the modern urban artist while simultaneously transcending that medium by employing it in the service of more "classical" concerns of portraiture. He has confounded artists and critics of both camps: the representational group that graffiti artists condescendingly describe as "didactic" or "simple," as well as the graf artists who the more traditionally minded art cognoscenti patronize with terms like "untrained," "naïve" or—God forbid—"urban." Yet he is subverting the motives and conceits of them all, and, in his own humble way, he knows it.

THE ARTIST

MIXING THINGS UP

Most any kind of furniture can find a comfortable place in Harlem Style. But it is fundamentally about individual pieces and the synthesis between them, rather than ensembles or suites. After that, the two most important ideas are accessibility and function.

Designers think of furniture much in the same way that painters or sculptors think about composition and form. Furniture is used as building blocks, to bring an anchoring square shape to a room filled with frilly friezes and details for example, or, conversely, to bring curved lines to a room that is all right angles. Many freely move among stylistic periods and genres, contemporizing a space by adding modern touches, but avoiding dating it or appearing trendy by also including things that are grounded in the past.

"I pick great pieces of furniture that don't necessarily belong to the same time period, but that relate to each other," explains Eve Robinson. "I don't think things have to be really expensive. I don't care where it's from or who it's attributed to or whether it's important. I just look at the lines of the piece; it's about shape and color and interest. I don't like a room that's all

This two-tiered table from Roderick Shade's African Impressions Collection is inspired by the Dogon tribe, which uses softly curved silhouettes with straight lines and chamfered edges in many of its designs.

FURNITURE

In Harlem Style, what matters when choosing furniture is how each piece interacts with others in the room, as well as with the architecture that envelops them. ABOVE: This three-door cabinet with carved knobs from Roderick Shade's African Impressions Collection actually takes its cue from an original Gilbert Rhode design. The gently swooping scalloped façade brings curved lines to a room filled with right angles.

RIGHT: In Yolanda Ferrell-Brown's Harlem townhouse on 104th Street, a voluminous antique claw-foot chair with carved lion-head arms proves a more interesting partner for an art deco desk than a chair from the same period or style would be.

Biedermeier or all French 1940s. That's just not interesting. I'd rather mix Anglo-Indian with Empire."

Again, we return to contrasts. Boxy, chunky, or sculptural pieces, says Clodagh, are attractive in urban settings. "It has to do with the ephemeral quality of life. You need to find your grounding." But these mix with smooth, streamlined, highly evolved pieces. Primal textures and shapes dovetail with high-gloss surfaces and stylized lines. An ornate French gold-leaf chair may share space with a Dakota Jackson leather chaise of simple, deconstructed design. A Moroccan tray table inlaid with mother-of-pearl may sit next to a Mies van der Rohe daybed or a Barcelona chair. There is a deliberate fusion of styles, materials, and grades of finish. Contemporary furniture is punctuated with antique traditional furniture and with tribal and hand-wrought pieces. Casualness alloys with formality. And Harlem Style rooms strike a harmonious balance between substance and volume on the one hand and delicacy and lightness on the other.

Yolanda Ferrell-Brown's dining room combines a 1920s bar with a '60s Lucite and glass table and a '40s chandelier. Christopher Coleman finds interest in mixing "a Victorian chest with more streamlined furniture." He explains, "The mix of materials and styles is, to me, what makes it urban. I like found objects, things you pick up in the street and use as a base for a table or make into a lamp. I like glitz with garbage."

The very nature of urban living also makes many of us more conscious about how we compose our spaces. The fact that the majority of apartments are smaller requires more editing of our interiors. And the up-to-the-second trendiness of city life means we are constantly re-evaluating possessions in light of new developments in design, art, and fashion.

"The notion of viewing objects in the round is a modernist one," believes Tony Whitfield. "It's not that Victorian idea of a sofa against a wall. Furniture takes on a very three-dimensional presence...And people are more discerning about what they put in their urban environments. Country houses may stay the same for longer periods of time. It's like fashion—people in urban settings see themselves more in relation to the modern components of their contemporary culture. They see their space as a palette that reflects who and where they are at a particular place and time. They see themselves as collectors, and they're aware of the gallery, the museum setting, so the space has to be clear to showcase their objects."

Yet, even though some designers like John Barman may favor furniture that "is more styled—deco, Regency, Empire and fancier antiques," Harlem Style doesn't lean toward the precious or favor museum rooms.

"I think the living room has finally become the living room, rather than the room roped off with velvet cords that your friends see on the way to another room," says Darryl Carter. "The furniture there has to make people feel they can not only sit in the room, but sit down in it. You want them to feel comfortable about putting a drink on a surface without worrying about ruining it."

As with any post-war design aesthetic, accessibility and function are paramount concerns. Ideally, a space should be kid-, cat-, and dog-friendly. And it should convey a lived-in, worked-in quality. "People's lifestyles have changed," explains Richard Mishaan. "Affluence is no longer defined by having an English Country look or that French Provincial thing. It's become more of an expression of who they are, of their life. There's a sophisticated ease in design that has to incorporate the elegance that city lifestyle will require, but it also has to fit in kids and dogs and home offices—all the components of modern living."

Duality of purpose is just as important. A work desk can be in a dining room. And why should a chair be confined to one spot rather than moving between living and dining rooms as needed? Small, mobile furniture is desirable: African spider web tables, teak hour-glass stools from the Philippines or Vietnam, Indonesian drum tables, and Chinese porcelain garden seats can be picked up, moved around and pressed into service as table surface or seating. All manner of

FURNITURE

PREVIOUS PAGE: **The soft curves of Danish chairs from the 1950s and a drum table blend so harmoniously into the straight edges of this Dallas loft designed by Gary Jackson that the skyline outside the windows becomes the major attraction.** RIGHT: **In John Barman's apartment, he creates interest by bringing seemingly disparate pieces together. While most of the furnishings are contemporary, the wire-base ottomans add a sense of lightheartedness more reminiscent of the party-happy 1960s. They're multifunctional, too, and could just as easily serve as occasional tables.**

small occasional furniture adds versatility to any grouping. "The majority of Americans don't have huge spaces," notes Eve Robinson, "so they want things to work for them in different ways, things that have wheels or that fold." Christopher Coleman admits to "putting wheels and swivels on everything. I like to be able to slide a chair over to where you need it. That suits the more casual lifestyle of modern living."

Larger, less mobile pieces can be used in ways for which they may not have been originally intended. A console table can double as a sideboard, a large table can be pressed into service as a desk, and a chest, while offering attractive storage, can double as a coffee table. And even beyond the individual pieces in a space, the whole room can often adapt to many functions. "The functions of rooms are not hidden or segregated," says Tony Whitfield. "You might find a bathtub in the middle of a room or a bathroom without a door. There's a titillation with the dissolution of privacy."

Some traditional functions of a room may be completely ignored altogether. "In the city, people tend to go out more, so use of space is different," says John Barman. "A smaller apartment usually can do without a dining area. It can be turned into an office or a den." Kitchens, points out Clodagh, have become more prominent gathering places because "we lack a sense of community in the city, and the kitchen becomes a place where you can create an environment of your own for a while. It's about sharing rituals."

FURNITURE | In the Todd Hase Furniture store in SoHo, a tuxedo-arm sofa, deco-inspired Lucite table (both Hase designs) and a massive Chinese red lacquer armoire seem as if they've always belonged together because they emit a lively energy that comes from the play between line, color, and materials.

PLUG IT IN, TURN IT ON, SHOW IT OFF

Reiterating the anti-Victorian impulse from which Harlem Style sprang, these rooms emphasize the activities performed there rather than attempt to hide or compartmentalize work spaces or entertainment areas. TVs, computers, and other technologies are figured into a room's overall scheme and left exposed. "There was a tendency to hide monitors and screens," notes Tony Whitfield. "With the slimming of components, that has changed. The expression of those functions has become so minimal, so you can show it without it calling attention to itself. Sound and light systems are built into the architecture of a room."

Some designers are more fond of technology's place in the general scheme of a room than others. Richard Mishaan, for instance, is a big fan. "Technology is so much a part of modern day life," he says. "Built-in stereos, TVs, conferencing equipment—they're not even considered forward anymore. Five-year-olds are computer literate. Technology used to be something so assaulting or 'wow.' I love the look of it now. It was ugly; now it's good-looking."

Modern components are so trim-lined these days that you hardly notice the plasma TV screen above the antique dentist's table that serves as a bar in Eve Robinson's installation for the 2000 Kips Bay Showhouse. The sense of harmony is enhanced by grid patterns on floor and ceiling and a barely perceptible grid hand-stitched onto the upholstered walls.

On the other hand, "I'm of the hide-it school," admits Darryl Carter, whose take on contemporary urban style is more traditional. "I put plasma screens under split canvases that look like linear paintings."

But no matter where you stand on this issue, it seems clear that the trend will only continue to grow as we become increasingly wired and technology reaches into almost every aspect of daily life. Most of us would be no more likely to trade in our computers for old manual typewriters than we would our PalmPilots for the leather-bound day planners that seemed to connote executive cachet barely ten years ago. That growth is exponential, becoming more accelerated with each passing hour.

This growth begets an aesthetic all its own—clean, black, digitized, and compact—that in turn influences contemporary design of every discipline.

TECHNOLOGY

In this room by Courtney Sloane, technology blends seamlessly into the function of the space. It is both prominent, as with the widescreen television, and semidisguised, as with the audio components below the screen. Technology here not only expresses the connectedness of the client to the worlds of media, fashion, and entertainment, but it imparts an aesthetic of its own (black, compact, and straight-edged) that informs the entire decor of the room.

objects and accessories

A GLOBAL EXCHANGE

The American theme-minded decorating habits of the 1950s encouraged us to appoint rooms head-to-toe in French Provincial or Spanish Colonial or Danish Modern, right down to the paintings, ashtrays, and vases. This approach had the effect of denying personal identity. It was decorating for the masses in which the individual became lost or completely obscured. Of course, this arose from industrialization and from the American penchant for valuing "new" over "old."

Somewhere along the line though, most perceptively in the 1960s, we began to realize the emotional vacuity of that approach, and we longed for both the hand of the craftsperson and for objects that spoke to our inner lives and aspirations. Unlike the 1960s however, when the countercultural backlash against industrialization was practically phobic and spawned truckloads of round brown pottery and macramé plant hangers, the new sensibility is more democratic.

In Courtney Sloane's apartment, a chair and mirror by Cheryl Riley, a teak table from Indonesia, paintings by Chris Ofili, a zebra-covered ottoman, and a kuba-cloth pillow.

What most sets Harlem Style apart from other contemporary urban design aesthetics is its democratic amalgam of objects from many different cultures. LEFT: In Greenwich Village, artist Barton Lidice Beneš lives amid a stunning array of tribal arts from India, the American Southwest, Africa, and most every continent on the globe. RIGHT: The concept of multiculturalism springs vividly to life in these two jam-packed views of Ethnix Tribal Arts gallery in Manhattan.

There is a place for the high-tech, production-line Nambé bowl as well as the hand-woven sweetgrass basket, for the halogen lamp as well as the floating aromatherapy candles, for the John Singer Sargent Iris-print as well as the ceremonial Yoruba mask.

Where Harlem Style is concerned, you could also say that the anything-goes blending of objects rose partly out of necessity. As blacks came out of slavery, walls were often inventively adorned with what was affordable and at hand. Often, what was affordable and at hand was a hodgepodge. The black migration also brought a variety of African, American Southern, and Caribbean styles into the mix—masks, shields and beadery, Southern quilts and baskets, colorful painted sculpture made of recycled metal drums, Haitian voodoo flags.

During the Harlem Renaissance, the new American black identity ensured that the most popular ethnic accents were African, and many Harlem Style interiors still have a lot of African touches. But today the global nature of economies and of urban societies the world over have put us in daily contact with the beautiful handiwork of India, the Middle East, Japan, China, and Latin America, to name just a few.

What the Harlem Renaissance did, believes Tony Whitfield, was drive a wedge into the thinking that Anglo European art and style were the pinnacles of human creative achievement. It opened the world to a re-evaluation of all cultures. "During the Harlem Renaissance, there was a fascination with the African American as

OBJECTS The things we possess speak singularly of our background and experiences and, in that way, become the most personal statements in a room. The art and objects on Mario Aranda's blue wall chronicle travels, relationships, and interests, and reflect the multi-ethnic mélange that defines him as a person.

Harlem Originals

The road to Harlem is more circuitous for some than for others. In the case of the three men who own this house, the journey snaked from Manhattan's southernmost financial district to Brooklyn to New Jersey before arriving uptown at Edgecombe Avenue.

The trio had been living around Lincoln Center, which, says one, "had become more a tourist destination than a neighborhood." They put their place on the market and began looking for a potential replacement. Some 250 prospects later, our gentlemen remained homeless.

Then one day they visited this late 1800s brownstone in Harlem. The building was hardly promising at first glance. It had been split up into a dozen or so units with kitchenettes, and all the walls, cabinets, and moldings had been painted white. Still, the friends realized the building's potential. They bought it, then hired a plumber to reroute and repair pipes, and a contractor to rethink the space for their needs.

A major concern was how to house their collection of Native American pottery, numbering more than 900 pieces. Beginning in the 1970s, they trekked annually to Santa Fe each season to indulge their love of music at the outdoor Santa Fe Opera. They met a dealer who specialized in Native American ceramics and, through their relationship with him, began visiting the various pueblos that produced pottery around Santa Fe.

Eventually, their new interest displaced their *al fresco* devotions to Wagner, Verdi, and Puccini altogether.

Most of that collection, which was largely documented in *Fourteen Families of Pueblo Pottery* by Rick Dillingham, the ceramic specialist who educated them, landed in the front living room of their Harlem home. Cream-colored Hopi pottery crowds onto shelves with black-on-black pieces from the Santa Clara, San Idelfonso, and other pueblos. There are paintings by Native American artist friends. One of the gentlemen also collects glass. All these are displayed against Navajo red walls.

Their acquisitions don't end with pottery and glass. There are collections of music memorabilia, costume designs and—well, that's a story for another day....

being 'exotic.' It had to do with the core of that culture being inaccessible. I don't think we have that anymore. We're easily connected through the Internet and multinational entities. The reality of travel and the dispersion of people across the globe have made us aware of a range of traditions and, in turn, a range of approaches to modernism. People take part in cultures that once seemed totally out of the question, and with that has come an appreciation of original cultures and artifacts."

For Darryl Carter, "The ethnic influence contemporizes an environment," because it represents the way we live now and the connection we have to global societies. Mario Aranda adds, "I am a mix of races and cultures—Mexican, Chinese, Scottish, English, with traces of Jewish—and I think, in the urban context, a lot of people are facing that situation. It's about finding your place in an environment, about drawing from different cultural sources and synthesizing."

It's also a modernist attitude, believes Aranda. "The idea of 'primitive' as a derogatory term is fairly recent. It actually means 'original' or 'basic.' It doesn't mean underdeveloped. It's true that it's not necessarily refined, but it's not lower on some evolutionary scale. It cuts clear, and that's what modernist sensibility is about. Ostentation is about an object pretending to be something it's not, which is the opposing tendency of modernism." The Eameses, he points out, collected Indian block-print fabrics, African masks, and pre-Columbian artifacts. "They were interested in everything from a piece of driftwood to a textile. They were looking for pure form, and the origins of pure form come from everywhere."

The objects and accessories in Harlem Style interiors become a statement about being "connected" in every way—to world cultures, fashion, contemporary art, technology, and good design. These connections speak of our urbanity, worldliness, and sophistication.

OBJECTS

A West African granary door brings an ethnic reference to Darryl Carter's Washington, D.C. bedroom, contemporizing what is at heart a deconstructed, traditional American environment.

LEFT: Yolanda Ferrell-Brown collects art by African-American painters and sculptors, which is displayed among furnishing that are basically traditional in feel. Leopard upholstery adds another cultural reference.
RIGHT: The nineteenth-century architectural elements of Terry C. Lane's Harlem brownstown are a backdrop for contemporary furniture and objects that are inspired by African design, such as the lamp on this side table. Designer Marc Anderson also added a quasi-Asian touch with simple linen shades.

EARTHLY CONNECTIONS

Clodagh takes the interior use of natural materials quite literally. In addition to using natural fibers and wood, she builds in a wall-length shelf for living wheat grass, dirt and root structure intact, which becomes an indispensable linear element of the décor.

Harlem Style interiors are part exterior in the sense that they bring in elements of the outdoors. We've seen this in the widespread use of natural grasses in furniture and on floor- and wallcoverings. Straw, jute, seagrass, rattan peel, raffia, bamboo, water hyacinth, abaca, hemp, twine, and other natural fibers become fringe, upholstery, webbing, furniture, and wallcoverings.

This, too, is a modern, twentieth-century development that began with exposure to Eastern cultures, but really gained popularity with the re-evaluation of African art and design. More recently, specifically during the 1960s, the popularity of Eastern religions opened the door wider for Asian aesthetics that incorporated natural fibers in everything from room screens to roofing. Today, the rage for feng shui, the ancient Chinese art of placement, has made natural fibers still more revered, along with other manifestations of nature inside the home, like water fountains.

Tony Whitfield is a vocal advocate for this return to natural materials in the home. Particularly after September 11, 2001, he notices the need among his students at Parsons School of Design, as well as by the world at large, "to reassess the level of consumption, which had become a defining force for America. That will have a radical impact on our lives if it holds," he predicts. And that impact will be reflected in a "different understanding of urbanism, nature, and the relationship between the two."

It is, in fact, already apparent. His students are opting out of school programs that are sponsored by many luxury goods companies, programs that would normally be a budding designer's dream. It's part of what has lately been called a "paradigm shift" in the way people think about the world and their place in it. "There has already been a movement away from the millennial role that plastic and synthetics had acquired and a shift to a more contemporary approach to natural materials," says Whitfield. "The technological world is a cold environment; it doesn't give back in any meaningful way. So there's a movement toward integrating that technology into an environment that is warmer and more welcoming. Natural materials do that very easily. There's also a way of using technology to create materials that have familiar properties, to produce flooring out of bamboo, or fine, extraordinarily pliable textiles from metal, or turn soy into resins. These all reintegrate themselves into the environment in some way."

NATURAL MATERIALS

In this Dallas loft's Japanese-style dining room, Gary Jackson mixes the industrial products of human labor (a massive steel table and poured concrete) with natural materials (sand and dried grasses) that speak of the leisure time humankind spends on the enjoyment of Earth's great gifts.

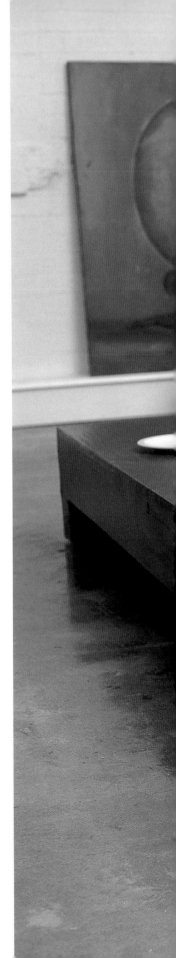

NATURAL MATERIALS

The operative word in the phrase "natural materials" is "natural"—meaning the raw, unpolished condition in which we find these elements in their native surroundings. LEFT: For a bathroom in the Harlem brownstone of Terry C. Lane, designer Marc Anderson eschewed glazed tile in favor of 12-inch honed slate squares to cover the floor and walls. RIGHT: Clockwise from top right, grass cloth wallpaper from Sonia's Place; liana cane fiber from Guyana is woven into a chair design by Tony Whitfield, head of the Parsons product design program; beautifully grained golden marble tile from Ann Sacks; a woven sisal rug from Patterson, Flynn & Martin.

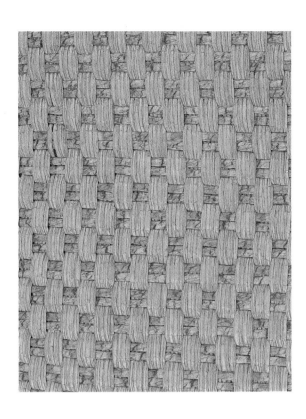

ABOVE: **Tony Whitfield's award-winning Socabot rocker woven from liana cane, a natural fiber from Guyana.** OPPOSITE: **For Terry C. Lane's dining room in Harlem, designer Marc Anderson could have used an ornate table that more closely matched the period architectural detail, but he chose this massive, blocky piece instead, to convey a sense of wood in a more natural state that is closer to its origins.**

Those are the basic elements of Harlem Style. You begin with a fairly neutral setting—through a muted, largely monochromatic palette and an awareness of architectural structure—then add touches of drama and contrast by using metallics, color, a variety of juxtaposed textures (both natural and synthetic), and patterns. Finally, you fill that setting with furniture, art, and objects that embody the concept of contemporary urban living: that is, of its connectedness to other cultures and customs, to its awareness of past and present, to fashion and technology, to a more casual sort of sophistication that incorporates both work and family. You keep it real with natural materials and reminders of the ecology that supports the very cities in which we live. Through these methods—which can be adopted in infinite degrees and combinations—Harlem Style enables you to create an interior that is uniquely your own, a sanctuary that reflects your particular fusion of interests and experiences, and presents them in a modern, stylish context.

putting it together

Now we understand the various components of Harlem Style and what each contributes, on its own, to a room. We've seen that, as distinct and separate elements, they can be elastically interpreted and applied, adapted in greater or lesser degree according to the specifics of a space, and the personalities of those who inhabit it. We've also glimpsed a narrowed view of how these elements interact with each other in small details, corners of rooms, and vignettes.

In the pages that follow, we've pulled back to examine the way various elements work in concert within the context of entire rooms. Again, this is a very elastic proposition. The work of Clodagh will not resemble the work of Christopher Coleman. Mario Aranda's use of strong color will contrast visibly with the down-to-earth, monochromatic palette of Marc Anderson. Technology will be conspicuously absent in a Darryl Carter interior, while it will make a brash, cutting-edge statement in one created by Courtney Sloane. And Sharne Algottson's apartment will exude a more handmade sort of comfort than a John Barman interior, which will feel more sleek and glamorous.

Yet, if you look closely, all of the rooms pull together several elements of Harlem Style. That is the beauty of contemporary urban design in general: its infinite breadth and versatility. It draws on an ever-expanding vocabulary of decorative genres, cultures, art, fashion, technological innovation, and current events. Each designer approaches a space with a particular sensibility that is informed by the way he or she absorbs and reacts to the varied stimuli present in the urban landscape. But the end result always displays a sense of worldliness and sophistication that is particular to city life.

Come home to Harlem Style.

PREVIOUS PAGE AND LEFT:

This room by Roderick Shade exemplifies many basic principles of Harlem Style. The home of Sharon Horowitz is designed to showcase her collection of African art and artifacts. Shade starts off with a white and beige backdrop, then adds textures that complement and enhance the art—a white chenille sofa, gold leaf on the coffee table, kuba cloth pilows. The tactile effect of natural elements like cowry shells, wood, and woven grasses is highlighted against more refined, polished surfaces and forms.

In Roderick Shade's design for a guest suite in the 2000 Kips Bay Showhouse, he employs unexpected juxtapositions for dramatic effect—mudcloth is placed against silk, modern art (by noted black painters such as Romare Bearden, Alma Thomas, Norman Lewis, and Raymond Barthé) is paired with African sculpture, boldness of pattern adds excitement to a soothingly earthy palette, and shiny surfaces contrast with matte.

Designer Michael Cooper's townhouse on St. Nicholas Avenue in Harlem was gutted and refurbished into a multifunctional space that could serve both living and working needs, as well as be rented out occasionally for fashion, interior, and product photography. It was sparely decorated to make the changing functions of every room easy to accomplish with a minimum of fuss. The objects reflect his mixed-race heritage; they blend artifacts that are identifiably of African descent with traditional and contemporary furniture that is Western. Rugs are by Patterson, Flynn & Martin.

LEFT: In designer Sharne Algotsson's Philadelphia living room, glazed ocher walls with accents of rust, red, beige, and brown combine with wicker, sisal, cotton, and velvet to convey the rustic elegance of the Central and East African landscape. ABOVE: In her bedroom, soft colors and gold accents are reminiscent of North African caravans traveling desert routes to sell their treasures. Symbols stenciled on the walls represent reverence for the past (the Sankofa heart) and patience and faithfulness (the Nsoroma star).

To this Manhattan penthouse of an African-American record executive, Clodagh brings her usual sensitivity for natural materials and organic forms paired with contemporary industrial materials. Wood and natural fibers permeate her furniture and fabric choices. These are mixed with polished plaster and embossed steel. Highly stylized furniture in curvy, swooping shapes bring softness to a boxy room in accordance with the basic feng shui principles to which designer and client both subscribe. African influences are stated subtly, as with the pulls on the cabinet against the back wall and in various patterns around the room.

Clodagh's respect for the handmade is surely the reason this art and craft collector selected her to design this home. Her use of a warm monochromatic palette allows the boldness of color, pattern, and form inherent in the art, textiles, and objects to command undistracted attention. The purity of materials—a core philosophy behind the creation of contemporary crafts—is palpable. Immediately upon entering the room, one senses the honesty of hand-carved wood, cast glass, forged iron, and hand-loomed carpets.

Architect Marc Anderson makes even period surroundings feel contemporary. LEFT: The task was easier in the upper apartment of his own renovated East Harlem church since it was basically a clean-lined, box-shaped interior, devoid of Gothic detail, that was carved out of what was once vaulted open space. With its Barcelona chairs, Mies van der Rohe chaise, and graphic modern art, it could be a SoHo loft. RIGHT: In Terry C. Lane's 121st Street Harlem home, Anderson achieved a modern feel using color and high-design Italian furniture, which works surprisingly well with the Old Harlem splendor of the woodwork.

LEFT: Anderson's approach to the vast space of the church's first floor was to treat it like an industrial loft that happened to have Gothic arches (pared down to simple, curved wood lines surrounded by clean white walls) and a cathedral ceiling (brought down to human scale by painting it a deep, dark brown). Then he warmed the space with natural fibers and primitive art.

ABOVE: In Terry C. Lane's den, a cappuccino-colored wall brings out the richness of period woodwork. Stools covered in kuba cloth and a lithograph of Frederick Douglass, the great black journalist and statesman, pay homage to Harlem's African history.

In Dallas, Gary Jackson created a spare, modern loft that is at once contemporary and timelessly elegant by using a monochromatic palette, simple forms, and natural materials. An almost ascetic compositional restraint is balanced with the bold hues and imagery of the painting, and with the luxurious silvery shimmer of the sheer curtain that partially covers it. Industrial materials like chrome and iron are brought down to earth by the introduction of natural elements such as sand in the table insets.

Washington, D.C.-based designer Darryl Carter has a more conservative take on Harlem Style. ABOVE: In this bedroom, modernism's affection for purity of line and minimalist composition is balanced by the warm paint tone of the wall, classical shapes, and ethnic artifacts. RIGHT: In this conversation between the past and the present, the old-fashioned formality of Louis furniture is unbuttoned—relaxed by an abstract Cuban canvas, rustic Chinese table, and the bold graphics of a zebra rug.

Harlem Originals

"There are people who are furious with me because this was a Victorian house," says Joan MacGregor. "But there wasn't a lot of detail left, so I wasn't really pressed to go with a period.

We preserved what we could—moldings, banisters, floors—but our life, which has been largely in Maine, is what influenced us."

Mrs. MacGregor's Maine cottage aesthetic, transplanted to an 1898 brownstone on 144th Street in Harlem, runs as deep as the ocean. She and her husband, Roderick, established The Lobster Place, a wholesale and retail shellfish business, in a small storefront on Amsterdam Avenue in 1973 (located today in lower Manhattan's Chelsea Market complex). For years, the Long Island natives traveled between the Big Apple and the Pine Tree State, where they still keep a family home, raising three daughters and a son. Perhaps not coincidentally, their son entered the Coast Guard and, upon finishing his service, intends to go into the family business.

To Harlem's landlubber cosmopolitanism, the MacGregors have brought a seafaring consciousness. Mrs. MacGregor calls her decorating style "Early Miscellaneous." It was cobbled together by shopping at secondhand furniture stores in upper Manhattan and mixing in pine antiques from Maine. Most of the accessories relate to the lobstering life—lighthouses, tiny boats, old kerosene lanterns used by wives to guide their men in from sea, an anchor. Even the toile on the armchairs is indirectly connected to that world—specifically, the tendency of fishermen to be raconteurs. "Obviously it's French and doesn't relate particularly to Maine," admits Mrs. MacGregor, "but I like the storytelling quality of the toile designs."

Conversely, other artifacts—birdhouses, candlesticks—speak to the precious value fishing families place, because of the perils of the trade, on the safety and comforts of home. It is, in fact, Harlem's substantial moorings as a safe community that attracted the MacGregors. "We didn't move here for political reasons," she explains. "It's a wonderful neighborhood, a solid neighborhood."

LEFT: **In the 1998 Kips Bay Showhouse, the woven wood wall of this room by Eve Robinson is at once dramatic and soothing in its basket-weave simplicity. Sophisticated furnishings make it stylish, but natural elements like the seagrass rug keep it from becoming too high-style.**

RIGHT: **In Courtney Sloane's Greenwich Village apartment, her blend of exposed construction, luxurious and common materials, smooth and rough textures, and African accents results in an energetic, layered urban look that is down to earth, yet worldly.**

Christopher Coleman demonstrates deftness for mixing patterns and combining colors. The thought of bringing together blocks of solid primary hues (on pillows and the two-toned chair), stripes (on the rug and curtains), geometrics (on pillows), and retro-style fabric (on armchairs) might worry most clients. Yet by going out on a limb and teetering on the edge of confusion, he brings humor and a contemporary flair to a very staid, and potentially austere, living room.

LEFT: Christopher Coleman takes a totally different approach from that of the room on the preceding page. Pattern is minimal and bold color is practically nonexistent. Instead, interest springs from the dialogue between rounded edges and straight angles, and from the textures of lustrous wood, glazed ceramic, linen, and velvet.
RIGHT: No one employs the glamorous componenent of Harlem Style more effectively than John Barman. This bedroom is very high-style, and looks like something out of 1930s or '40s New York. But the spareness of the space and its use of modern art also give it a contemporary urban resonance.

ABOVE: **At the 2000 Kips Bay Showhouse, Richard Mishaan fused natural materials and a palette of earth tones with contemporary furniture and chairs that evoked the shapes of those one might have found in a turn-of-the-century Parisian cafe.**

RIGHT: **At Mishaan's Manhattan store, the emphasis is clearly on line and a mix of materials—chrome, marble, Lucite, and wood. Live goldfish in glass cylinders atop the coffee table take the idea of bringing nature indoors to its most literal conclusion.**

Fabric by Kravet

resources

DESIGNERS

ALTERNATIVE DESIGN
Courtney Sloane, Cheryl Riley
21 W. 16th St.
New York, NY 10011
(646) 230-7222
www.alternativedesign.com

M. ANDERSON DESIGN, INC.
Marc Anderson
1432 Lexington Ave.
New York, NY 10128
(212) 426-3801

JOHN BARMAN
500 Park Ave., 14F
New York, NY 10022
(212) 838-9443

CIELO VIVO
Mario Aranda
1252 N. Milwaukee Ave.
Chicago, IL 60622
(773) 782-9643
cielovivo@aol.com

CLODAGH DESIGN INTERNATIONAL
670 Broadway, 4th Floor
New York, NY 10012
(212) 780-5300
www.clodagh.com

CHRISTOPHER COLEMAN
70 Washington St.
Brooklyn, NY 11201
(718) 222-8984
ccoleman1005@hotmail.com

FERRELL-BROWN DESIGN, INC.
Yolanda Ferrell-Brown
319 W. 104th St.
New York, NY 10025
(212) 865-2401

INSIDE DESIGN
Sharne Algotsson
1245 Medary Ave.
Philadelphia, PA 19141
(215) 224-7808
www.insidedesignltd.com

JACKSON IVEY-JACKSON
Gary Jackson
2917-B Elm St.
Dallas, TX 75226
(214) 742-6200
www.jacksonivey-jackson.com

RICHARD MISHAAN DESIGN
150 E. 58th St., 22nd Floor
New York, NY 10155
(212) 223-7502

EVE ROBINSON ASSOCIATES, INC.
2112 Broadway, Suite 403
New York, NY 10023
(212) 595-0661

RODERICK N. SHADE, INC.
P.O. Box 1797
New York, NY 10026
(212) 681-7942
www.roderickshade.com

TONY WHITFIELD
398 Dean St.
Brooklyn, NY 11217
(718) 638-4514

RETAIL STORES · GENERAL

ARTISTIC TILE
79 Fifth Ave.
New York, NY 10003
(212) 727-9331

ETHNIX TRIBAL & AFRICAN ARTS
636 Broadway
New York, NY 10012
(212) 614-6610
www.ethnix.com
Museum quality tribal art, primarily from Africa, but also from Southeast Asia, South America and other regions. Jewelry, furniture, masks, sculpture, beaded works, baskets, textiles, some rugs.

TODD HASE FURNITURE, INC.
261 Spring St.
New York, NY 10013
(212) 334-3568

HOMER
939 Madison Ave.
New York, NY 10019
(212) 744-7705
www.homerdesign.com
Richard Mishaan designs, as well as Italian glass, European lighting, vintage and contemporary furniture, carpets, accessories.

KUBATANA MODERNE
1831 Peachtree Rd., N.E.
Atlanta, GA 30309
(404) 355-5764
www.kubatana.com
High-design furniture in a minimalist environment, mixed with contemporary art from around the world and museum-quality tribal pieces.

MATERIAL CULTURE
4700 Wissahickon Ave., Suite 101
Philadelphia, PA 19144
(215) 849-8030
www.materialculture.com
Assoso furniture from Ghana mixed with contemporary accessories and Tibetan carpets.

**MOSAIC ANTIQUE &
CONTEMPORARY DESIGN**
122 Hudson St.
New York, NY 10013
(646) 613-8570
www.interiorsbymosaic.com

FRANCE: **CONCEPT ETHNIC**
5 Quai de Conti
75006 Paris
(01) 56 24 43 92
Furniture from the end of the nineteenth century, the 1940s

and contemporary pieces, as well as its own design collection. African art, furniture, handmade African fabrics.

ANN SACKS TILE
5 East 16th St.
New York, NY 10003
(212) 463-8400
Tile, stone, bath fixtures: New York and nationwide.

USONA HOME FURNISHINGS
223 Market St.
Philadelphia, PA 19106
(215) 351-9160
www.usonahome.com
Contemporary European furniture mixed with antique and modern art and artifacts from Africa and Asia, as well as fur accessories.

RETAIL STORES · HARLEM

THE BROWNSTONE
2032 Fifth Ave.
New York, NY 10027
(212) 996-7980
Several businesses in one building, including the full interior design services of Design Schemes, African art and objects, and more.

DJEMA IMPORTS
70 W. 125th St.
New York, NY 10027
(212) 289-3842
www.djemaimports.com
A huge assortment of printed African textiles, mudcloth, and kuba cloth. Custom service for pillow covers, bags, garments, and other items.

KAARTA IMPORTS & EXPORTS
121 W. 125th St.
New York, NY 10027
(212) 866-6289
Yards and yards of African fabric from all over the continent piled as high as the ceiling and crammed into a tiny space.

MALCOLM SHABAZZ HARLEM MARKET
102 W. 116th St.
New York, NY 10026
Open 7 days a week. African textiles of every variety, beads and shells, basketry, and other objects sold by vendors from the whole of the African continent.

SCOTTY'S NEW AND USED FURNITURE
5 Hancock Pl.
New York, NY 10027
New, used and antique furniture from various eras, plus custom upholstery, in the heart of Harlem. Scotty is a Harlem institution.

TO THE TRADE SHOWROOMS

DONGHIA FURNITURE/TEXTILES LTD.
485 Broadway
New York, NY 10003
(212) 925-2777
www.donghia.com
High-end contemporary furniture, fabrics in every color, pattern and weave, wallcoverings.

KRAVET FABRICS
225 Central Ave. South
Bethpage, NY 11714
(516) 293-2000
www.e-designtrade.com
A large assortment of African-inspired fabrics, as well as textured weaves, silks, prints, and more.

PATTERSON, FLYNN & MARTIN
979 Third Ave.
New York, NY 10022
(212) 688-7700
High-end and custom floor-coverings from around the world. Schumacher fabrics also available.

SONIA'S PLACE
979 Third Ave., 10th Floor
New York, NY 10022
(212) 355-5211
Wallcoverings, fabrics, and trims of all types.

BIBLIOGRAPHY

Watson, Steven. *The Harlem Renaissance: Hub of African-American Culture*, 1920-1930. New York: Pantheon Books, 1995.

Lewis, David Levering. *When Harlem Was in Vogue*. New York: Penguin Books, 1997.

Campbell, Mary Schmidt. *Harlem Renaissance: Art of Black America*. (With essays by David Driscoll, David Levering Lewis and Deobrah Willis Ryan.) New York: Harry N. Abrams, Inc., 1994.

Newman, Richard. *African American Quotations*. New York: The Oryx Press, 2000.

Constant, Caroline. *Eileen Gray*. London: Phaidon Press Limited, 2000.

PHOTO CREDITS |

Pages 10–11: Photo courtesy of the Schomburg Center for Research in Black Culture; 14–15: photo by Jonn Coolidge; 16, 20: courtesy of the Schomburg Center for Research in Black Culture; 22–23: courtesy of the Museum of the City of New York, The Byron Collection; 25: photo by James VanDerZee, courtesy of the Studio Museum in Harlem, © Donna Mussenden VanDerZee; 26–27: first published in *L'Illustration*, courtesy of the Smithsonian Institution/Cooper-Hewitt, National Design Museum; 28–29: courtesy of the Schomburg Center for Research in Black Culture; 32, 44: photo by Jonn Coolidge; 47: photo by Jason Hughes, Hughes Photography; 48–49: photo by Max Hirshfeld; 59: photo by Peter Vitale, courtesy of John Barman; 61: photo by Keith Scott Morton, courtesy of Clodagh; 62: photo by Andrew Bordwin; 66: photo by Peter Vitale, courtesy of John Barman; 70: photo by Kate Roth; 74–75: photo by Keith Scott Morton, courtesy of Clodagh; 90-91: photo by Andrew Bordwin; 94: photo by Kate Roth; 108: Jason Hughes, Hughes Photography; 110–111: photo by Peter Vitale, courtesy of John Barman; 114: reprinted by permission of *House Beautiful*, copyright © August 2000, Hearst Communications, Inc. All rights reserved. Thibault Jeanson, photographer; 116–117: photo by Dub Rogers, courtesy of Courtney Sloane; 119: photo by Minh+Wass Photography; 122–123: photo by Kate Roth; 126: photo by Max Hirshfeld; 131: photo by Daniel Aubrey, courtesy of Clodagh; 132–133: photo by Jason Hughes, Hughes Photography; 135 (bottom right), 136: photos by Michael Canahuate, courtesy Tony Whitfield; 142, 143: photos by Bill Geddes; 148–149, 150–151: photos by Daniel Aubrey, courtesy of Clodagh; 156–157: photo by Jason Hughes, Hughes Photography; 158–159: photos by Robert Brantley, Delray Beach, FL copyright © 2001 *Florida Design*, Boca Raton, FL; 162: photo by Pieter Estersohn; 163: photo by Minh+ Wass Photography; 164–165: photo by Andrew Bordwin; 166: photo by John Heil; 167: photo by Peter Vitale, courtesy of John Barman; 168: photo by Peter Pierce, courtesy of Richard Mishaan.

Fabric by Kravet

EDITED BY MARISA BULZONE

DESIGNED BY ALEXANDRA MALDONADO

GRAPHIC PRODUCTION BY KIM TYNER

00285 8713